50 Canadian Restaurant Lunch Recipes for Home

By: Kelly Johnson

Table of Contents

- Montreal Smoked Meat Sandwich
- Butter Chicken Poutine
- Nova Scotia Lobster Roll
- Alberta Beef Burger
- PEI Mussels in White Wine
- Quebecois Tourtière
- Bannock with Wild Berry Compote
- Canadian Caesar Salad
- Smoked Salmon Bagel
- Bison Sloppy Joes
- Maple Glazed Ham Sandwich
- Clam Chowder
- Grilled Cheese with Maple Bacon
- Corn Chowder with Shrimp
- BeaverTail Pizza
- Wild Mushroom Soup
- Turkey Cranberry Panini
- Roasted Root Vegetable Salad
- Maple Mustard Chicken Wrap
- Salmon Quiche
- Pulled Pork Sandwich with Coleslaw
- Classic Fish and Chips
- Sweet Potato and Black Bean Burrito
- Cider-Glazed Pork Tacos
- Butternut Squash and Sage Risotto
- Chicken and Leek Pie
- Veggie-stuffed Empanadas
- Roast Beef and Horseradish Sandwich
- Atlantic Salmon Salad
- Stuffed Cornish Hen
- Canadian Club Sandwich
- Tomato and Basil Bruschetta

- Potato and Chive Fritters
- Teriyaki Chicken Skewers
- Crab Cakes with Lemon Aioli
- Shepherd's Pie
- BBQ Chicken Quesadilla
- Beet and Goat Cheese Salad
- Lamb and Mint Burgers
- Ginger Beef Stir-Fry
- Spinach and Feta Stuffed Chicken
- Blackened Tilapia Tacos
- Roasted Veggie and Hummus Wrap
- Spicy Butternut Squash Soup
- Pear and Gorgonzola Salad
- Chicken Pot Pie
- Maple Bacon Brussels Sprouts
- Poutine with Pulled Pork
- Cucumber and Dill Sandwiches
- Duck Confit Sandwich

Montreal Smoked Meat Sandwich

Ingredients:

- 1 lb Montreal smoked meat, sliced (can be bought from a deli or specialty store)
- 2 slices rye bread
- 2 tablespoons mustard (yellow or deli mustard)
- Pickles (optional, for serving)

Instructions:

1. **Preheat**: If you have a sandwich press or panini maker, preheat it according to the manufacturer's instructions. If not, a skillet or grill pan will work.
2. **Prepare the Meat**: Heat the Montreal smoked meat slices in a skillet over medium heat until warmed through. You can steam it if you prefer a more authentic texture.
3. **Toast the Bread**: Lightly butter the outside of each slice of rye bread. Toast them on a skillet or in a sandwich press until golden brown and crispy.
4. **Assemble the Sandwich**: Spread mustard on the inside of each slice of toasted rye bread. Layer the warmed Montreal smoked meat evenly on one slice of bread.
5. **Complete**: Top with the other slice of bread. Press down gently.
6. **Serve**: Cut the sandwich in half if desired and serve with pickles on the side.

Enjoy your homemade Montreal Smoked Meat Sandwich!

Butter Chicken Poutine

Ingredients:

For the Butter Chicken:

- 1 lb boneless, skinless chicken thighs or breasts, cut into bite-sized pieces
- 2 tablespoons vegetable oil
- 1 onion, finely chopped
- 3 cloves garlic, minced
- 1 tablespoon ginger, minced
- 1 tablespoon ground coriander
- 1 tablespoon ground cumin
- 1 teaspoon turmeric
- 1 teaspoon garam masala
- 1 can (14 oz) tomato sauce
- 1 cup heavy cream
- 2 tablespoons butter
- Salt and pepper to taste
- Fresh cilantro, chopped (for garnish)

For the Poutine:

- 1 lb frozen or homemade french fries
- 1 cup cheese curds (white cheddar or similar)
- Fresh cilantro, chopped (for garnish)

Instructions:

1. **Prepare the Butter Chicken:**
   - Heat vegetable oil in a large skillet over medium heat. Add the chopped onion and cook until soft and translucent, about 5 minutes.
   - Add the garlic and ginger, cooking for an additional 1 minute.
   - Stir in the ground coriander, cumin, turmeric, and garam masala. Cook for 1-2 minutes until fragrant.
   - Add the chicken pieces and cook until they are no longer pink on the outside, about 5-7 minutes.
   - Pour in the tomato sauce and bring to a simmer. Cook for 10-15 minutes, or until the chicken is fully cooked and tender.
   - Stir in the heavy cream and butter, and cook for an additional 5 minutes until the sauce is thickened. Season with salt and pepper to taste.
   - Garnish with fresh cilantro.
2. **Prepare the Fries:**

- Cook the french fries according to package instructions or your preferred method (deep frying, baking, etc.) until crispy and golden brown.
3. **Assemble the Poutine:**
    - Place the hot fries on a serving plate or dish.
    - Evenly distribute the cheese curds over the fries.
    - Spoon the butter chicken and sauce over the fries and cheese curds.
4. **Garnish and Serve:**
    - Garnish with additional fresh cilantro if desired.
    - Serve immediately while hot.

Enjoy your Butter Chicken Poutine—a delicious blend of Canadian comfort food and Indian flavors!

Nova Scotia Lobster Roll

Ingredients:

- 1 lb lobster meat (cooked and chopped; fresh or thawed from frozen)
- 2 tablespoons mayonnaise
- 1 tablespoon lemon juice
- 1 tablespoon chopped fresh chives (or parsley)
- 1 teaspoon Dijon mustard
- Salt and freshly ground black pepper, to taste
- 4 top-split hot dog rolls or split-top rolls
- 2 tablespoons butter (for toasting the rolls)
- Lettuce leaves (optional, for lining the rolls)

Instructions:

1. **Prepare the Lobster Meat:**
   - If using whole lobsters, cook them in boiling water for about 8-10 minutes, then cool them quickly in an ice bath. Remove the meat from the shells and chop it into bite-sized pieces.
2. **Make the Lobster Filling:**
   - In a medium bowl, combine the mayonnaise, lemon juice, chopped chives, Dijon mustard, salt, and pepper.
   - Gently fold in the lobster meat until evenly coated with the dressing. Adjust seasoning to taste.
3. **Prepare the Rolls:**
   - Heat the butter in a skillet over medium heat. Carefully place the rolls in the skillet and toast them until golden brown on both sides, about 2-3 minutes per side.
4. **Assemble the Lobster Rolls:**
   - If using lettuce, line the inside of each toasted roll with a leaf or two.
   - Spoon the lobster mixture generously into each roll.
5. **Serve:**
   - Serve immediately while the rolls are still warm and crispy.

Enjoy your Nova Scotia Lobster Roll, a delicious taste of the Canadian maritime coast!

Alberta Beef Burger

Ingredients:

- 1 lb ground Alberta beef (preferably 80% lean, 20% fat)
- 1 tablespoon Worcestershire sauce
- 1 teaspoon garlic powder
- 1 teaspoon onion powder
- Salt and freshly ground black pepper, to taste
- 4 hamburger buns
- 4 slices cheddar cheese (optional)
- Lettuce leaves
- Tomato slices
- Red onion slices
- Pickles
- Ketchup, mustard, and mayonnaise (optional, for serving)

Instructions:

1. **Prepare the Beef Patties:**
    - In a large bowl, gently mix the ground beef with Worcestershire sauce, garlic powder, onion powder, salt, and pepper. Be careful not to overwork the meat to avoid tough burgers.
    - Divide the mixture into 4 equal portions and shape each portion into a patty about ¾ inch thick. Use your thumb to make a small indent in the center of each patty to help them cook evenly and avoid puffing up in the middle.
2. **Cook the Patties:**
    - Preheat your grill or skillet over medium-high heat. If using a grill, lightly oil the grates to prevent sticking.
    - Cook the patties for about 4-5 minutes per side for medium-rare, or longer if you prefer them more well-done. If using cheese, place a slice on each patty during the last minute of cooking and cover with a lid to melt.
3. **Toast the Buns:**
    - While the patties are cooking, toast the hamburger buns on the grill or in a skillet until golden brown.
4. **Assemble the Burgers:**
    - Spread your choice of condiments on the bottom half of each bun.
    - Place a cooked beef patty on each bun.
    - Top with lettuce, tomato slices, red onion slices, and pickles.
    - Add more condiments if desired, then place the top half of the bun on each burger.
5. **Serve:**

- Serve the Alberta Beef Burgers immediately with your favorite side dishes like fries or coleslaw.

Enjoy your hearty and flavorful Alberta Beef Burger!

PEI Mussels in White Wine

Ingredients:

- 2 lbs PEI mussels, cleaned and debearded
- 2 tablespoons olive oil
- 1 onion, finely chopped
- 3 cloves garlic, minced
- 1 cup dry white wine
- 1 cup chicken or vegetable broth
- 1 lemon, juiced
- 1 teaspoon dried thyme (or a few sprigs of fresh thyme)
- 1/4 cup chopped fresh parsley
- Salt and freshly ground black pepper, to taste
- 1/2 teaspoon red pepper flakes (optional, for a bit of heat)
- Crusty bread (for serving)

Instructions:

1. **Prepare the Mussels:**
   - Rinse the mussels under cold water, scrubbing the shells and removing any beards. Discard any mussels that are open and do not close when tapped.
2. **Cook the Aromatics:**
   - Heat the olive oil in a large pot or Dutch oven over medium heat.
   - Add the chopped onion and cook until softened, about 5 minutes.
   - Add the minced garlic and cook for an additional 1 minute until fragrant.
3. **Add Liquids and Seasonings:**
   - Pour in the white wine and chicken or vegetable broth. Bring to a simmer.
   - Add the lemon juice, thyme, and red pepper flakes if using. Stir to combine.
4. **Cook the Mussels:**
   - Add the cleaned mussels to the pot. Cover and cook for 5-7 minutes, or until the mussels have opened. Discard any mussels that remain closed.
5. **Finish the Dish:**
   - Stir in the chopped parsley. Season with salt and pepper to taste.
6. **Serve:**
   - Ladle the mussels and broth into bowls. Serve with crusty bread for soaking up the delicious broth.

Enjoy your PEI Mussels in White Wine, a delightful and easy seafood dish that brings a taste of the Atlantic coast to your table!

Quebecois Tourtière

Ingredients:

For the Filling:

- 1 lb ground pork
- 1/2 lb ground beef
- 1/2 lb ground veal (optional, can use more pork or beef if preferred)
- 1 onion, finely chopped
- 2 cloves garlic, minced
- 1 teaspoon dried thyme
- 1/2 teaspoon ground cinnamon
- 1/4 teaspoon ground cloves
- 1/4 teaspoon ground nutmeg
- 1/2 cup beef or chicken broth
- 1/2 cup mashed potatoes (cooked and cooled)
- Salt and freshly ground black pepper, to taste

For the Pie Crust:

- 2 1/2 cups all-purpose flour
- 1 teaspoon salt
- 1 cup (2 sticks) unsalted butter, chilled and cut into small pieces
- 6-8 tablespoons ice water

Instructions:

1. **Prepare the Pie Crust:**
    - In a large bowl, combine the flour and salt. Cut in the butter using a pastry cutter or your fingers until the mixture resembles coarse crumbs.
    - Gradually add the ice water, one tablespoon at a time, mixing until the dough just begins to come together.
    - Divide the dough in half, shape each half into a disk, wrap in plastic wrap, and refrigerate for at least 1 hour.
2. **Prepare the Filling:**
    - In a large skillet over medium heat, cook the ground pork, beef, and veal until browned and fully cooked, breaking up the meat with a spoon. Drain excess fat if necessary.
    - Add the chopped onion and garlic to the skillet and cook until softened, about 5 minutes.
    - Stir in the thyme, cinnamon, cloves, and nutmeg. Cook for an additional 2 minutes to allow the spices to meld.

- Add the broth and mashed potatoes, mixing until well combined. Cook until the mixture is thickened and most of the liquid has evaporated. Season with salt and pepper to taste. Let the filling cool slightly.

3. **Assemble the Pie:**
   - Preheat the oven to 375°F (190°C).
   - Roll out one disk of dough on a lightly floured surface to fit a 9-inch pie pan. Transfer the rolled dough to the pie pan and trim any overhanging edges.
   - Spoon the cooled filling into the pie crust and spread it out evenly.
   - Roll out the second disk of dough and place it over the filling. Trim, seal, and crimp the edges. Cut a few slits in the top crust to allow steam to escape.

4. **Bake:**
   - Brush the top crust with an egg wash (1 beaten egg mixed with 1 tablespoon of water) for a golden finish.
   - Bake in the preheated oven for 45-50 minutes, or until the crust is golden brown and the filling is bubbly.

5. **Cool and Serve:**
   - Let the tourtière cool for at least 15 minutes before slicing. This helps the filling set.

Enjoy your Quebecois Tourtière, a comforting and flavorful pie that's perfect for festive occasions or a hearty meal!

Bannock with Wild Berry Compote

Ingredients:

- 2 cups all-purpose flour
- 2 tablespoons baking powder
- 1/2 teaspoon salt
- 1/4 cup sugar (optional)
- 1/2 cup cold butter, cubed
- 3/4 cup milk (or buttermilk for a richer flavor)
- 1 large egg

Instructions:

1. **Preheat Oven**: Preheat your oven to 375°F (190°C). If you prefer, you can cook the bannock in a skillet over medium heat.
2. **Mix Dry Ingredients**: In a large bowl, whisk together the flour, baking powder, salt, and sugar (if using).
3. **Cut in Butter**: Add the cubed butter to the dry ingredients. Use a pastry cutter or your fingers to blend the butter into the flour until the mixture resembles coarse crumbs.
4. **Add Wet Ingredients**: In a separate bowl, whisk together the milk and egg. Pour this mixture into the dry ingredients and stir until just combined.
5. **Shape and Bake**: Turn the dough out onto a lightly floured surface and gently knead it a few times. Shape it into a round or square loaf, about 1-inch thick. Place the dough onto a baking sheet lined with parchment paper.
6. **Bake**: Bake for 20-25 minutes, or until the top is golden brown and a toothpick inserted into the center comes out clean. Let it cool slightly before slicing.

Wild Berry Compote:

Ingredients:

- 2 cups mixed wild berries (e.g., blueberries, raspberries, strawberries, blackberries)
- 1/4 cup sugar (adjust based on the sweetness of your berries)
- 1 tablespoon lemon juice
- 1 teaspoon cornstarch (optional, for thickening)
- 2 tablespoons water (if using cornstarch)

Instructions:

1. **Combine Ingredients**: In a medium saucepan, combine the berries, sugar, and lemon juice. Cook over medium heat, stirring occasionally, until the berries begin to break down and release their juices, about 5-7 minutes.

2. **Thicken (Optional)**: If you prefer a thicker compote, mix the cornstarch with the water to form a slurry. Stir this into the berry mixture and cook for an additional 1-2 minutes until the compote has thickened.
3. **Cool**: Remove from heat and let the compote cool slightly. It will continue to thicken as it cools.

Serve:

- Slice the warm bannock and serve with a generous spoonful of wild berry compote on top.

Enjoy your Bannock with Wild Berry Compote as a delicious treat for breakfast, brunch, or dessert!

Canadian Caesar Salad

Ingredients:

For the Salad:

- 1 large head of Romaine lettuce, washed and torn into bite-sized pieces
- 1 cup croutons (store-bought or homemade)
- 1/2 cup grated Parmesan cheese
- 2-3 strips of crispy bacon, crumbled (optional, but adds a nice Canadian touch)
- 1/4 cup thinly sliced red onion (optional)

For the Dressing:

- 1/2 cup mayonnaise
- 2 tablespoons lemon juice
- 2 tablespoons Dijon mustard
- 2 tablespoons Worcestershire sauce
- 1-2 cloves garlic, minced
- 1 tablespoon grated Parmesan cheese
- Salt and freshly ground black pepper, to taste

Instructions:

1. **Prepare the Dressing:**
   - In a medium bowl, whisk together the mayonnaise, lemon juice, Dijon mustard, Worcestershire sauce, minced garlic, and grated Parmesan cheese until smooth.
   - Season the dressing with salt and pepper to taste. Adjust the seasoning or lemon juice if needed. Refrigerate until ready to use.
2. **Prepare the Salad:**
   - In a large salad bowl, combine the torn Romaine lettuce with the croutons and grated Parmesan cheese.
   - If using, add the crumbled bacon and thinly sliced red onion.
3. **Toss and Serve:**
   - Drizzle the dressing over the salad and toss gently until the lettuce and croutons are evenly coated.
   - Serve immediately, garnishing with additional Parmesan cheese and freshly ground black pepper if desired.

Enjoy your Canadian Caesar Salad as a fresh and zesty accompaniment to any meal!

Smoked Salmon Bagel

Ingredients:

- 1 plain or everything bagel
- 2 tablespoons cream cheese
- 4-6 slices of smoked salmon
- 1/4 small red onion, thinly sliced
- 1 small cucumber, thinly sliced
- 1 tablespoon capers (optional)
- Fresh dill or chives, chopped (for garnish)
- Lemon wedge (for serving)
- Salt and freshly ground black pepper, to taste

Instructions:

1. **Toast the Bagel:**
     - Slice the bagel in half and toast it until golden brown. You can use a toaster or toast it in a skillet for extra crispiness.
2. **Spread the Cream Cheese:**
     - Once toasted, spread the cream cheese evenly over both halves of the bagel.
3. **Assemble the Toppings:**
     - Arrange the slices of smoked salmon over one half of the bagel.
     - Top with thin slices of red onion and cucumber.
     - Add capers if using, and sprinkle with fresh dill or chives.
4. **Season:**
     - Season with a pinch of salt and freshly ground black pepper to taste.
5. **Serve:**
     - Place the other half of the bagel on top to complete the sandwich. Serve with a lemon wedge on the side for a squeeze of fresh lemon juice.

Enjoy your Smoked Salmon Bagel as a luxurious and satisfying breakfast or brunch!

Bison Sloppy Joes

Ingredients:

- 1 lb ground bison
- 1 tablespoon olive oil
- 1 onion, finely chopped
- 1 bell pepper, finely chopped (red or green)
- 2 cloves garlic, minced
- 1 cup tomato sauce
- 1/4 cup ketchup
- 2 tablespoons Worcestershire sauce
- 1 tablespoon Dijon mustard
- 1 tablespoon brown sugar
- 1 teaspoon smoked paprika
- 1/2 teaspoon ground cumin
- 1/2 teaspoon dried oregano
- Salt and freshly ground black pepper, to taste
- 4 hamburger buns (preferably whole wheat or brioche)
- Optional toppings: shredded cheese, pickles, sliced jalapeños

Instructions:

1. **Cook the Bison:**
    - Heat olive oil in a large skillet over medium heat.
    - Add the ground bison and cook, breaking it up with a spoon, until browned and cooked through. Drain any excess fat if needed.
2. **Add Vegetables:**
    - Add the chopped onion and bell pepper to the skillet with the bison. Cook for about 5 minutes, or until the vegetables are softened.
    - Stir in the minced garlic and cook for an additional 1 minute until fragrant.
3. **Prepare the Sauce:**
    - Add the tomato sauce, ketchup, Worcestershire sauce, Dijon mustard, brown sugar, smoked paprika, cumin, and oregano to the skillet. Stir to combine.
4. **Simmer:**
    - Reduce the heat to low and let the mixture simmer for about 10-15 minutes, or until the sauce has thickened and the flavors have melded together. Stir occasionally.
5. **Season:**
    - Season with salt and pepper to taste.
6. **Prepare the Buns:**
    - While the filling simmers, toast the hamburger buns in a toaster or on a skillet until lightly golden.

7. **Assemble the Sloppy Joes:**
    - Spoon the bison mixture onto the bottom half of each toasted bun.
    - Add any optional toppings like shredded cheese or pickles.
8. **Serve:**
    - Place the top half of the bun over the filling and serve hot.

Enjoy your Bison Sloppy Joes for a hearty, flavorful meal with a lean twist!

Maple Glazed Ham Sandwich

Ingredients:

For the Maple Glaze:

- 1/4 cup pure maple syrup
- 2 tablespoons Dijon mustard
- 1 tablespoon brown sugar
- 1 tablespoon apple cider vinegar
- 1/2 teaspoon ground black pepper

For the Sandwich:

- 4 slices of hearty bread (such as sourdough or whole grain)
- 4-6 slices of deli ham (or leftover baked ham)
- 4 slices of Swiss cheese or your favorite cheese
- 2 tablespoons mayonnaise
- 2 tablespoons whole-grain mustard (optional)
- 1 cup baby spinach or arugula (optional)
- Pickles or apple slices (optional, for garnish)

Instructions:

1. **Make the Maple Glaze:**
    - In a small saucepan, combine the maple syrup, Dijon mustard, brown sugar, apple cider vinegar, and black pepper.
    - Heat over medium heat, stirring occasionally, until the mixture comes to a simmer and slightly thickens, about 3-4 minutes.
    - Remove from heat and let it cool slightly.
2. **Prepare the Ham:**
    - Preheat a skillet over medium heat.
    - Brush or spoon some of the maple glaze onto the ham slices.
    - Cook the ham slices in the skillet for 1-2 minutes per side, or until warmed through and slightly caramelized.
3. **Toast the Bread:**
    - While the ham is cooking, toast the bread slices in a toaster or on a separate skillet until golden brown.
4. **Assemble the Sandwich:**
    - Spread mayonnaise (and whole-grain mustard, if using) on one side of each slice of toasted bread.
    - Place a slice of cheese on the bottom half of each sandwich.
    - Top with the warm, glazed ham slices.
    - Add a handful of baby spinach or arugula if desired.

5. **Finish and Serve:**
    - Top with the other slice of bread.
    - Serve immediately, garnished with pickles or apple slices if desired.

Enjoy your Maple Glazed Ham Sandwich—a delightful blend of sweet and savory flavors with a touch of elegance!

Clam Chowder

Ingredients:

- 4 slices bacon, chopped
- 1 medium onion, finely chopped
- 2 cloves garlic, minced
- 2 stalks celery, chopped
- 1 medium carrot, peeled and diced
- 1/4 cup all-purpose flour
- 2 cups clam juice (or seafood broth)
- 1 cup milk
- 1 cup heavy cream
- 2 cups diced potatoes (peeled or unpeeled, as preferred)
- 1 can (about 6.5 oz) chopped clams, with juice (or fresh clams, if available)
- 1 bay leaf
- 1 teaspoon dried thyme
- 1/2 teaspoon dried parsley (or 1 tablespoon fresh parsley, chopped)
- Salt and freshly ground black pepper, to taste
- 2 tablespoons butter
- Optional: 1/2 cup frozen or fresh corn kernels
- Fresh parsley or chives, for garnish

Instructions:

1. **Cook the Bacon:**
   - In a large pot or Dutch oven, cook the chopped bacon over medium heat until crispy. Remove the bacon with a slotted spoon and set aside, leaving the bacon drippings in the pot.
2. **Sauté the Vegetables:**
   - Add the chopped onion, garlic, celery, and carrot to the pot with the bacon drippings. Cook over medium heat until the vegetables are softened, about 5-7 minutes.
3. **Make the Roux:**
   - Stir in the flour and cook for 1-2 minutes to make a roux. This will help thicken the chowder.
4. **Add Liquids and Potatoes:**
   - Gradually add the clam juice (or seafood broth), stirring constantly to avoid lumps. Bring to a simmer.
   - Add the diced potatoes, bay leaf, thyme, and dried parsley. Simmer until the potatoes are tender, about 15-20 minutes.
5. **Add Clams and Cream:**

- Stir in the chopped clams (with their juice) and the heavy cream. Simmer gently for 5 minutes. If using corn, add it at this point.
6. **Season and Finish:**
    - Remove the bay leaf. Season with salt and freshly ground black pepper to taste.
    - Stir in the butter until melted and incorporated.
7. **Serve:**
    - Ladle the chowder into bowls. Garnish with the cooked bacon and fresh parsley or chives.

Enjoy your homemade Clam Chowder—a warm and hearty soup perfect for any time of year!

Grilled Cheese with Maple Bacon

Ingredients:

- 4 slices of bread (sourdough, whole grain, or your favorite type)
- 4 tablespoons unsalted butter, softened
- 4-6 slices of your favorite cheese (such as sharp cheddar, Gruyère, or Swiss)
- 4 slices of bacon
- 2 tablespoons pure maple syrup
- Optional: 1 tablespoon Dijon mustard or mayonnaise (for additional flavor)

Instructions:

1. **Prepare the Bacon:**
   - Preheat your oven to 375°F (190°C).
   - Place the bacon slices on a baking sheet lined with parchment paper.
   - Brush the bacon slices with maple syrup.
   - Bake in the preheated oven for 15-20 minutes, or until crispy and caramelized. Flip the bacon halfway through the cooking time. Remove from the oven and set aside on paper towels to drain excess fat.
2. **Prepare the Bread:**
   - Spread butter evenly on one side of each slice of bread.
   - If using, spread a thin layer of Dijon mustard or mayonnaise on the unbuttered side of two of the bread slices.
3. **Assemble the Sandwiches:**
   - Place the cheese slices on the unbuttered side of the bread slices (2 slices of bread per sandwich).
   - Lay the crispy maple bacon on top of the cheese.
   - Top with the remaining slices of bread, buttered side facing out.
4. **Grill the Sandwiches:**
   - Heat a skillet or griddle over medium heat.
   - Place the sandwiches in the skillet and cook for 3-4 minutes per side, or until the bread is golden brown and the cheese is melted. Press down slightly with a spatula to ensure even grilling.
5. **Serve:**
   - Remove the sandwiches from the skillet and let them cool for a minute before slicing.
   - Serve warm.

Enjoy your Grilled Cheese with Maple Bacon, a deliciously sweet and savory take on a classic comfort food!

Corn Chowder with Shrimp

Ingredients:

- 2 tablespoons butter
- 1 medium onion, finely chopped
- 2 cloves garlic, minced
- 2 celery stalks, chopped
- 1 medium carrot, peeled and diced
- 1 red bell pepper, diced (optional)
- 4 cups fresh or frozen corn kernels (about 4-5 ears of corn or 2 cups frozen)
- 3 cups chicken or vegetable broth
- 1 cup milk
- 1 cup heavy cream
- 1 pound large shrimp, peeled and deveined, tails removed
- 2 tablespoons all-purpose flour
- 1 teaspoon dried thyme
- 1 bay leaf
- 1/2 teaspoon paprika
- Salt and freshly ground black pepper, to taste
- 2 tablespoons fresh parsley or chives, chopped (for garnish)
- Optional: 1/2 cup diced potatoes or diced bacon

Instructions:

1. **Prepare the Base:**
    - In a large pot or Dutch oven, melt the butter over medium heat.
    - Add the chopped onion, garlic, celery, and carrot (and bell pepper, if using). Cook until the vegetables are softened, about 5-7 minutes.
2. **Add Flour and Corn:**
    - Stir in the flour and cook for 1-2 minutes to create a roux, which will help thicken the chowder.
    - Add the corn kernels and cook for another 2 minutes.
3. **Add Liquids and Seasonings:**
    - Gradually pour in the chicken or vegetable broth, stirring constantly to avoid lumps.
    - Add the milk, heavy cream, thyme, bay leaf, paprika, and salt and pepper.
    - Bring the mixture to a simmer and cook for about 15 minutes, or until the chowder is slightly thickened and the flavors have melded together.
4. **Cook the Shrimp:**
    - In the last 5 minutes of cooking, add the shrimp to the chowder.
    - Cook until the shrimp are pink and opaque, about 3-5 minutes.
5. **Optional Additions:**

- If using diced potatoes, add them along with the broth and cook until tender.
- If adding bacon, cook it separately until crispy, then crumble it and add to the chowder at the end.

6. **Finish and Serve:**
    - Remove the bay leaf.
    - Adjust seasoning with more salt and pepper if needed.
    - Garnish with fresh parsley or chives.

Enjoy your Corn Chowder with Shrimp—a hearty and flavorful soup that's perfect for any time of year!

BeaverTail Pizza

Ingredients:

For the Dough:

- 1 1/2 cups warm water (110°F/45°C)
- 2 teaspoons active dry yeast
- 1 tablespoon sugar
- 3 1/2 cups all-purpose flour
- 1 teaspoon salt
- 2 tablespoons olive oil

For the Toppings:

- 1/2 cup tomato sauce or pizza sauce
- 1 cup shredded mozzarella cheese
- 1/2 cup cooked bacon, crumbled (optional)
- 1/2 cup sliced pepperoni or cooked sausage (optional)
- 1/4 cup caramelized onions (optional)
- 1/4 cup sliced mushrooms (optional)
- 2 tablespoons honey
- 2 tablespoons melted butter
- 1/2 teaspoon ground cinnamon
- 2 tablespoons granulated sugar
- Optional: fresh basil or parsley for garnish

Instructions:

1. **Prepare the Dough:**
    - In a small bowl, dissolve the sugar in warm water and sprinkle the yeast on top. Let it sit for about 5 minutes, or until frothy.
    - In a large bowl, combine the flour and salt. Make a well in the center and pour in the yeast mixture and olive oil.
    - Mix until the dough begins to come together, then knead on a floured surface for about 5-7 minutes until smooth and elastic. You can also use a stand mixer with a dough hook.
    - Place the dough in a lightly oiled bowl, cover with a damp cloth, and let it rise in a warm place for about 1 hour, or until doubled in size.
2. **Prepare the Pizza Base:**
    - Preheat your oven to 475°F (245°C) and place a pizza stone or baking sheet inside to heat up.
    - Punch down the dough and divide it into 2-3 equal portions, depending on the size of the BeaverTail pizzas you want.

- Roll out each portion into an oval or "beaver tail" shape on a floured surface, about 1/4 inch thick.
3. **Assemble the Pizza:**
    - Carefully transfer the rolled-out dough onto a piece of parchment paper or a floured pizza peel.
    - Spread a thin layer of tomato sauce over the dough, leaving a small border around the edges.
    - Sprinkle with mozzarella cheese and add any additional savory toppings like bacon, pepperoni, caramelized onions, or mushrooms.
4. **Bake the Pizza:**
    - Transfer the pizza (with parchment paper if using) onto the preheated pizza stone or baking sheet.
    - Bake for 10-12 minutes, or until the crust is golden brown and the cheese is bubbly and melted.
5. **Finish with Sweet Toppings:**
    - While the pizza is baking, mix the granulated sugar and ground cinnamon together in a small bowl.
    - As soon as the pizza comes out of the oven, brush it with melted butter and drizzle with honey.
    - Sprinkle the cinnamon sugar mixture over the top while it's still warm.
6. **Serve:**
    - Garnish with fresh basil or parsley if desired.
    - Slice and serve warm.

Enjoy your BeaverTail Pizza—a delightful combination of sweet and savory flavors with a crispy, chewy crust!

Wild Mushroom Soup

Ingredients:

- 2 tablespoons olive oil
- 1 medium onion, finely chopped
- 2 cloves garlic, minced
- 2 celery stalks, chopped
- 1 medium carrot, peeled and diced
- 1 pound mixed wild mushrooms (such as shiitake, porcini, cremini, or morel), cleaned and sliced
- 1 cup cremini or button mushrooms, sliced
- 4 cups vegetable or chicken broth
- 1 cup heavy cream
- 2 tablespoons all-purpose flour (optional, for thickening)
- 1 tablespoon fresh thyme leaves (or 1 teaspoon dried thyme)
- 1 bay leaf
- Salt and freshly ground black pepper, to taste
- 2 tablespoons unsalted butter (optional, for extra richness)
- 1/4 cup dry white wine (optional)
- Fresh parsley or chives, chopped, for garnish

Instructions:

1. **Prepare the Vegetables:**
   - Heat the olive oil in a large pot or Dutch oven over medium heat.
   - Add the chopped onion, garlic, celery, and carrot. Cook until the vegetables are softened and the onion is translucent, about 5-7 minutes.
2. **Cook the Mushrooms:**
   - Add the wild mushrooms and cremini mushrooms to the pot. Cook, stirring occasionally, until the mushrooms are tender and have released their moisture, about 8-10 minutes.
   - If using white wine, pour it in now and cook for an additional 2-3 minutes, allowing the alcohol to evaporate.
3. **Add Broth and Seasonings:**
   - Stir in the flour (if using) and cook for 1-2 minutes to form a roux. This will help thicken the soup.
   - Add the vegetable or chicken broth, thyme, and bay leaf. Bring the mixture to a simmer and cook for about 15 minutes, allowing the flavors to meld together.
4. **Blend the Soup:**
   - Remove the bay leaf.

- Use an immersion blender to puree the soup until smooth, or carefully transfer the soup in batches to a blender and blend until smooth. If you prefer a chunkier texture, blend only part of the soup.
5. **Add Cream and Finish:**
    - Return the soup to the pot if needed and stir in the heavy cream. Heat through, but do not boil.
    - Stir in the butter (if using) for extra richness.
    - Season with salt and freshly ground black pepper to taste.
6. **Serve:**
    - Ladle the soup into bowls and garnish with fresh parsley or chives.

Enjoy your Wild Mushroom Soup—rich, creamy, and full of the deep, savory flavors of wild mushrooms!

Turkey Cranberry Panini

Ingredients:

- 4 slices of crusty bread (such as ciabatta, sourdough, or whole grain)
- 1 cup cooked turkey, sliced or shredded
- 1/2 cup cranberry sauce (homemade or store-bought)
- 4 slices of Swiss cheese or your favorite cheese (such as provolone or cheddar)
- 2 tablespoons mayonnaise
- 1 tablespoon Dijon mustard
- 2 tablespoons butter, softened
- Optional: fresh spinach or arugula, for added crunch and freshness

Instructions:

1. **Prepare the Bread:**
    - Preheat a panini press or a skillet over medium heat.
    - Spread the softened butter evenly on one side of each slice of bread.
2. **Assemble the Panini:**
    - On the non-buttered side of two of the bread slices, spread a thin layer of mayonnaise and Dijon mustard.
    - Layer the sliced turkey evenly over the mayonnaise side.
    - Spoon cranberry sauce over the turkey.
    - Place a slice of cheese on top of the cranberry sauce.
    - If using, add a handful of fresh spinach or arugula on top of the cheese.
    - Top with the remaining slices of bread, buttered side facing out.
3. **Grill the Panini:**
    - If using a panini press: Place the sandwiches in the press and close it. Cook according to the manufacturer's instructions, usually for 3-5 minutes, until the bread is golden brown and the cheese is melted.
    - If using a skillet: Place the sandwiches in the skillet and press down slightly with a spatula. Cook for about 3-4 minutes per side, or until the bread is golden brown and the cheese is melted. You can use another skillet or a weight (like a can) to press the sandwiches down to achieve a nice grill mark.
4. **Serve:**
    - Remove the panini from the press or skillet and let them cool for a minute before slicing.
    - Cut in half and serve warm.

Enjoy your Turkey Cranberry Panini—a perfect blend of savory turkey, sweet cranberry sauce, and melted cheese, all pressed between crispy, buttery bread!

Roasted Root Vegetable Salad

Ingredients:

For the Salad:

- 3 medium carrots, peeled and cut into bite-sized pieces
- 2 medium parsnips, peeled and cut into bite-sized pieces
- 1 small sweet potato, peeled and cut into bite-sized pieces
- 1 medium red onion, peeled and cut into wedges
- 2 tablespoons olive oil
- Salt and freshly ground black pepper, to taste
- 1 teaspoon dried thyme or rosemary (or 1 tablespoon fresh, chopped)
- 4 cups mixed greens (such as spinach, arugula, or baby kale)
- 1/4 cup crumbled feta cheese or goat cheese
- 1/4 cup toasted nuts (such as walnuts, pecans, or almonds)
- Optional: 1/4 cup dried cranberries or pomegranate seeds for added sweetness and color

For the Dressing:

- 3 tablespoons olive oil
- 1 tablespoon balsamic vinegar
- 1 tablespoon Dijon mustard
- 1 teaspoon honey or maple syrup
- Salt and freshly ground black pepper, to taste

Instructions:

1. **Roast the Vegetables:**
    - Preheat your oven to 425°F (220°C).
    - On a large baking sheet, toss the carrots, parsnips, sweet potato, and red onion with olive oil, salt, pepper, and dried thyme or rosemary.
    - Spread the vegetables in a single layer on the baking sheet.
    - Roast for 25-30 minutes, or until the vegetables are tender and caramelized, turning them halfway through cooking for even roasting. Remove from the oven and let cool slightly.
2. **Prepare the Dressing:**
    - In a small bowl or jar, whisk together the olive oil, balsamic vinegar, Dijon mustard, honey or maple syrup, salt, and pepper until well combined.
3. **Assemble the Salad:**
    - In a large bowl, toss the mixed greens with a small amount of the dressing.
    - Top with the roasted vegetables.

- Sprinkle with crumbled feta or goat cheese, toasted nuts, and optional dried cranberries or pomegranate seeds.
4. **Serve:**
    - Drizzle the remaining dressing over the salad just before serving, or serve it on the side.
    - Toss gently to combine.

Enjoy your Roasted Root Vegetable Salad—a warm and satisfying dish that's perfect for a hearty lunch or as a side for dinner!

Maple Mustard Chicken Wrap

Ingredients:

For the Chicken:

- 1 pound boneless, skinless chicken breasts or thighs
- 2 tablespoons olive oil
- 1/4 cup pure maple syrup
- 1/4 cup Dijon mustard
- 1 tablespoon whole-grain mustard (optional, for extra texture)
- 2 cloves garlic, minced
- 1 teaspoon dried thyme or rosemary
- Salt and freshly ground black pepper, to taste

For the Wraps:

- 4 large tortillas or wraps
- 1 cup shredded lettuce or mixed greens
- 1/2 cup sliced cucumber
- 1/2 cup shredded carrots
- 1/2 cup sliced red bell pepper
- 1/4 cup sliced red onion
- 1/4 cup crumbled feta cheese or shredded cheddar cheese (optional)

Instructions:

1. **Prepare the Chicken:**
   - In a bowl, whisk together the maple syrup, Dijon mustard, whole-grain mustard (if using), minced garlic, dried thyme or rosemary, salt, and pepper.
   - Place the chicken breasts or thighs in a resealable bag or shallow dish and pour the marinade over them. Marinate in the refrigerator for at least 30 minutes, or up to 4 hours for more flavor.
2. **Cook the Chicken:**
   - Preheat a grill or skillet over medium heat and brush with olive oil.
   - Remove the chicken from the marinade and cook for 5-7 minutes per side, or until the chicken is cooked through and has an internal temperature of 165°F (74°C). The cooking time will vary depending on the thickness of the chicken.
   - Remove from heat and let the chicken rest for a few minutes before slicing into strips.
3. **Assemble the Wraps:**
   - Warm the tortillas in a dry skillet or microwave to make them more pliable.
   - Lay out each tortilla and spread a layer of shredded lettuce or mixed greens in the center.

- Top with sliced cucumber, shredded carrots, sliced red bell pepper, sliced red onion, and crumbled feta or shredded cheddar cheese (if using).
    - Arrange the sliced chicken on top of the vegetables.
4. **Wrap and Serve:**
    - Fold the sides of the tortilla over the filling, then roll it up from the bottom to form a wrap.
    - Slice in half if desired and serve immediately.

Enjoy your Maple Mustard Chicken Wraps—an easy and tasty meal that balances sweet and tangy flavors with fresh vegetables!

Salmon Quiche

Ingredients:

For the Crust:

- 1 1/2 cups all-purpose flour
- 1/2 teaspoon salt
- 1/2 cup cold unsalted butter, cut into small cubes
- 1/4 cup ice water (more if needed)

For the Filling:

- 1 tablespoon olive oil
- 1 small onion, finely chopped
- 1/2 cup chopped bell pepper (red, green, or yellow)
- 1 cup fresh or smoked salmon, skin removed and flaked
- 1 cup shredded cheese (such as Swiss, Gruyère, or cheddar)
- 4 large eggs
- 1 cup heavy cream or whole milk
- 1/2 teaspoon dried dill (or 1 tablespoon fresh dill, chopped)
- 1/2 teaspoon dried thyme
- Salt and freshly ground black pepper, to taste

Instructions:

1. **Prepare the Crust:**
    - Preheat your oven to 375°F (190°C).
    - In a medium bowl, combine the flour and salt. Cut in the cold butter using a pastry cutter or your fingers until the mixture resembles coarse crumbs.
    - Gradually add ice water, a tablespoon at a time, mixing until the dough just comes together. Avoid overworking the dough.
    - Press the dough into a 9-inch pie dish or tart pan, covering the bottom and sides evenly. Use a fork to prick the bottom of the crust.
    - Chill the crust in the refrigerator for 15 minutes.
2. **Blind Bake the Crust:**
    - Line the chilled crust with parchment paper and fill with pie weights or dried beans.
    - Bake in the preheated oven for 10 minutes. Remove the parchment paper and weights, and bake for an additional 5 minutes, or until the crust is lightly golden. Remove from the oven and set aside.
3. **Prepare the Filling:**

- Heat the olive oil in a skillet over medium heat. Add the chopped onion and bell pepper. Cook until the vegetables are softened, about 5 minutes. Remove from heat and let cool slightly.
- In a medium bowl, whisk together the eggs, cream or milk, dill, thyme, salt, and pepper.
- Stir in the cooked onion and bell pepper, flaked salmon, and shredded cheese.

4. **Assemble the Quiche:**
    - Pour the filling into the pre-baked crust, spreading it evenly.
5. **Bake the Quiche:**
    - Bake in the preheated oven for 30-35 minutes, or until the filling is set and the top is lightly golden.
    - Let the quiche cool for a few minutes before slicing.
6. **Serve:**
    - Serve warm or at room temperature. Garnish with additional fresh dill if desired.

Enjoy your Salmon Quiche—a perfect blend of creamy custard, rich salmon, and fresh vegetables in a flaky crust!

Pulled Pork Sandwich with Coleslaw

For the Pulled Pork:

Ingredients:

- 3-4 pounds pork shoulder (also called pork butt)
- 2 tablespoons olive oil
- 1 large onion, chopped
- 4 cloves garlic, minced
- 1 cup barbecue sauce (your favorite brand or homemade)
- 1/2 cup apple cider vinegar
- 1/2 cup chicken broth
- 1 tablespoon smoked paprika
- 1 tablespoon brown sugar
- 1 teaspoon ground cumin
- 1 teaspoon chili powder
- 1/2 teaspoon dried oregano
- Salt and freshly ground black pepper, to taste

Instructions:

1. **Prepare the Pork:**
   - Pat the pork shoulder dry and season all sides with salt and pepper.
   - Heat olive oil in a large skillet or Dutch oven over medium-high heat. Sear the pork on all sides until browned, about 5 minutes per side. Remove the pork and set aside.
2. **Cook the Pork:**
   - In the same skillet or Dutch oven, add the chopped onion and garlic. Cook until softened, about 5 minutes.
   - Stir in the barbecue sauce, apple cider vinegar, chicken broth, smoked paprika, brown sugar, cumin, chili powder, and oregano.
   - Return the pork to the pot, ensuring it's covered with the sauce mixture.
   - Cover and transfer to a preheated oven at 300°F (150°C) or cook on low in a slow cooker for 6-8 hours, or until the pork is tender and easily shreds with a fork.
3. **Shred the Pork:**
   - Remove the pork from the cooking liquid and shred it using two forks. Discard any large pieces of fat.
   - Return the shredded pork to the pot and mix with the sauce. Adjust seasoning with salt and pepper if needed.
4. **Prepare the Coleslaw:**

Ingredients:

- 1 small head of green cabbage, finely shredded
- 1 small head of red cabbage, finely shredded
- 2 large carrots, peeled and grated
- 1 cup mayonnaise
- 2 tablespoons apple cider vinegar
- 1 tablespoon Dijon mustard
- 1 tablespoon honey or sugar
- Salt and freshly ground black pepper, to taste
- Optional: 1/4 cup chopped fresh parsley or chives

Instructions:

1. **Prepare the Dressing:**
   - In a large bowl, whisk together the mayonnaise, apple cider vinegar, Dijon mustard, honey (or sugar), salt, and pepper.
2. **Combine the Coleslaw:**
   - Add the shredded green cabbage, red cabbage, and grated carrots to the bowl with the dressing.
   - Toss well to coat all the vegetables with the dressing.
   - Refrigerate for at least 30 minutes to allow the flavors to meld.
3. **Assemble the Sandwiches:**

Ingredients:

- 4-6 hamburger buns or sandwich rolls
- Pickles (optional, for topping)
- Additional barbecue sauce (optional)

Instructions:

1. **Toast the Buns:**
   - Toast the hamburger buns or sandwich rolls if desired, either in a toaster or under a broiler for a few minutes.
2. **Assemble the Sandwiches:**
   - Pile a generous portion of pulled pork onto the bottom half of each bun.
   - Top with a heaping spoonful of coleslaw.
   - Add pickles and extra barbecue sauce if desired.
   - Place the top half of the bun on the sandwich.
3. **Serve:**
   - Serve the pulled pork sandwiches immediately with your favorite sides.

Enjoy your Pulled Pork Sandwich with Coleslaw—a perfect blend of smoky, tangy, and crunchy flavors!

Classic Fish and Chips

Ingredients:

For the Fish:

- 4 large fish fillets (such as cod, haddock, or pollock), skinless and boneless
- 1 cup all-purpose flour, plus extra for dredging
- 1 cup cold sparkling water or beer (for a lighter batter, use sparkling water; for extra flavor, use beer)
- 1 teaspoon baking powder
- 1/2 teaspoon salt
- 1/2 teaspoon black pepper
- 1/2 teaspoon paprika (optional, for a hint of color)
- Vegetable oil, for frying

For the Chips:

- 4 large russet potatoes, peeled
- Salt, to taste
- Optional: malt vinegar or tartar sauce, for serving

Instructions:

1. **Prepare the Chips:**
    - Cut the peeled potatoes into thick slices or wedges, about 1/2 inch thick.
    - Place the cut potatoes in a bowl of cold water and soak for at least 30 minutes to remove excess starch. This helps make them crispier.
2. **Preheat the Oil:**
    - Heat a large pot or deep fryer with enough vegetable oil to submerge the chips and fish. Heat the oil to 325°F (165°C) for frying the chips and 375°F (190°C) for frying the fish.
3. **Cook the Chips:**
    - Drain and pat the potato slices dry with a clean towel.
    - Fry the potatoes in batches at 325°F (165°C) for about 4-5 minutes, until they are soft but not yet browned. Remove with a slotted spoon and drain on paper towels.
    - Increase the oil temperature to 375°F (190°C).
    - Return the potatoes to the hot oil and fry for an additional 2-4 minutes, or until they are golden and crispy. Remove and drain on paper towels. Season with salt immediately.
4. **Prepare the Batter:**
    - In a bowl, mix the flour, baking powder, salt, pepper, and paprika.

- Gradually whisk in the cold sparkling water or beer until the batter is smooth and thick enough to coat the back of a spoon.
5. **Cook the Fish:**
    - Pat the fish fillets dry with paper towels and season lightly with salt and pepper.
    - Dredge each fillet in a little flour, shaking off the excess. This helps the batter adhere better.
    - Dip the floured fillets into the batter, allowing any excess to drip off.
    - Carefully lower the battered fish into the hot oil and fry in batches until golden brown and crispy, about 5-7 minutes. The fish should be cooked through and have an internal temperature of 145°F (63°C).
    - Remove the fish with a slotted spoon and drain on paper towels.
6. **Serve:**
    - Serve the fish and chips hot, with optional malt vinegar or tartar sauce on the side.

Enjoy your Classic Fish and Chips—a satisfying combination of crispy, golden fish and fluffy fries, perfect for a traditional meal!

Sweet Potato and Black Bean Burrito

Ingredients:

For the Filling:

- 2 medium sweet potatoes, peeled and diced
- 1 tablespoon olive oil
- 1 teaspoon ground cumin
- 1 teaspoon paprika
- 1/2 teaspoon chili powder
- Salt and freshly ground black pepper, to taste
- 1 can (15 oz) black beans, drained and rinsed
- 1/2 cup corn kernels (fresh, frozen, or canned)
- 1/2 cup diced red bell pepper
- 1/4 cup chopped fresh cilantro (optional)

For the Burritos:

- 4 large flour tortillas (or whole wheat tortillas)
- 1 cup shredded cheese (cheddar, Monterey Jack, or your favorite cheese)
- 1 cup cooked rice (white, brown, or Spanish rice)
- 1/2 cup sour cream or Greek yogurt
- 1/2 cup salsa or pico de gallo
- Optional: avocado slices or guacamole, hot sauce, lime wedges

Instructions:

1. **Roast the Sweet Potatoes:**
    - Preheat your oven to 400°F (200°C).
    - Toss the diced sweet potatoes with olive oil, cumin, paprika, chili powder, salt, and pepper.
    - Spread the sweet potatoes in a single layer on a baking sheet.
    - Roast for 25-30 minutes, or until the sweet potatoes are tender and slightly caramelized. Stir halfway through cooking for even roasting.
2. **Prepare the Filling:**
    - In a large bowl, combine the roasted sweet potatoes, black beans, corn, diced red bell pepper, and chopped cilantro (if using). Mix well.
3. **Assemble the Burritos:**
    - Warm the tortillas in a dry skillet or microwave to make them more pliable.
    - Lay out each tortilla and spread a layer of cooked rice in the center.
    - Top with a generous portion of the sweet potato and black bean mixture.
    - Sprinkle with shredded cheese.

- Add a dollop of sour cream or Greek yogurt and a spoonful of salsa or pico de gallo.
- If desired, add avocado slices or guacamole.

4. **Wrap the Burritos:**
    - Fold the sides of the tortilla over the filling.
    - Roll up from the bottom to form a tight burrito.
    - If desired, you can lightly toast the burritos in a skillet over medium heat, seam side down first, until they are golden and crispy, about 2-3 minutes per side.

5. **Serve:**
    - Slice the burritos in half if desired and serve with additional salsa, hot sauce, lime wedges, or extra sour cream.

Enjoy your Sweet Potato and Black Bean Burrito—a flavorful and nutritious option that's perfect for a quick lunch or dinner!

Cider-Glazed Pork Tacos

Ingredients:

For the Pork:

- 1.5 to 2 pounds pork shoulder or pork butt, trimmed and cut into bite-sized pieces
- 1 tablespoon olive oil
- 1 medium onion, finely chopped
- 3 cloves garlic, minced
- 1 cup apple cider
- 2 tablespoons apple cider vinegar
- 1 tablespoon Dijon mustard
- 2 tablespoons brown sugar
- 1 teaspoon smoked paprika
- 1/2 teaspoon ground cumin
- 1/2 teaspoon ground cinnamon
- 1/2 teaspoon dried thyme
- Salt and freshly ground black pepper, to taste

For the Tacos:

- 8 small flour or corn tortillas
- 1 cup shredded cabbage or coleslaw mix
- 1/2 cup fresh cilantro, chopped
- 1 avocado, sliced
- 1 lime, cut into wedges
- Optional: salsa or pico de gallo, sour cream, pickled red onions

Instructions:

1. **Cook the Pork:**
    - Heat olive oil in a large skillet or Dutch oven over medium-high heat.
    - Add the pork pieces and sear until browned on all sides, about 5-7 minutes. Remove the pork from the skillet and set aside.
    - In the same skillet, add the chopped onion and cook until softened, about 5 minutes.
    - Add the minced garlic and cook for an additional 1 minute.
    - Stir in the apple cider, apple cider vinegar, Dijon mustard, brown sugar, smoked paprika, cumin, cinnamon, and thyme. Bring to a simmer.
    - Return the pork to the skillet and stir to coat with the sauce.
    - Reduce the heat to low, cover, and simmer for 1.5 to 2 hours, or until the pork is tender and easily shreds with a fork. Alternatively, you can cook the pork in a slow cooker on low for 6-8 hours.

2. **Prepare the Toppings:**
    - While the pork is cooking, prepare your taco toppings. Shred the cabbage or coleslaw mix, chop the cilantro, and slice the avocado. Cut the lime into wedges.
3. **Assemble the Tacos:**
    - Once the pork is tender, shred it using two forks and mix it with the cider glaze in the skillet.
    - Warm the tortillas in a dry skillet or microwave to make them pliable.
    - Place a portion of the cider-glazed pork in the center of each tortilla.
    - Top with shredded cabbage or coleslaw mix, chopped cilantro, and avocado slices.
    - Add optional toppings like salsa, sour cream, or pickled red onions if desired.
4. **Serve:**
    - Serve the tacos with lime wedges on the side for squeezing over the top.

Enjoy your Cider-Glazed Pork Tacos—tender, flavorful pork with a hint of sweetness from the cider, all wrapped up in a delicious taco!

Butternut Squash and Sage Risotto

Ingredients:

For the Roasted Butternut Squash:

- 1 small butternut squash, peeled, seeded, and cut into 1/2-inch cubes
- 2 tablespoons olive oil
- Salt and freshly ground black pepper, to taste
- 1/2 teaspoon ground cinnamon (optional, for extra warmth)

For the Risotto:

- 4 cups chicken or vegetable broth (preferably low-sodium)
- 1 tablespoon olive oil
- 1 small onion, finely chopped
- 2 cloves garlic, minced
- 1 1/2 cups Arborio rice
- 1/2 cup dry white wine (or extra broth if you prefer not to use wine)
- 1 cup freshly grated Parmesan cheese
- 1/4 cup chopped fresh sage (or 1 tablespoon dried sage)
- 2 tablespoons unsalted butter
- Salt and freshly ground black pepper, to taste
- Optional: additional Parmesan cheese and fresh sage for garnish

Instructions:

1. **Roast the Butternut Squash:**
   - Preheat your oven to 400°F (200°C).
   - Toss the butternut squash cubes with olive oil, salt, pepper, and ground cinnamon (if using).
   - Spread the squash in a single layer on a baking sheet.
   - Roast for 25-30 minutes, or until the squash is tender and caramelized, stirring halfway through cooking. Remove from the oven and set aside.
2. **Prepare the Broth:**
   - In a saucepan, keep the chicken or vegetable broth warm over low heat.
3. **Cook the Risotto:**
   - In a large skillet or saucepan, heat olive oil over medium heat.
   - Add the chopped onion and cook until softened and translucent, about 5 minutes.
   - Add the minced garlic and cook for an additional minute.
   - Stir in the Arborio rice and cook for 1-2 minutes, allowing the rice to toast slightly and absorb the flavors.
   - Pour in the white wine and cook, stirring frequently, until the wine is mostly absorbed.

4. **Add the Broth:**
    - Begin adding the warm broth to the rice, one ladleful at a time, stirring frequently and allowing each addition to be absorbed before adding the next. Continue this process until the rice is creamy and cooked to your desired level of doneness (usually about 18-20 minutes).
5. **Incorporate the Squash and Sage:**
    - Once the risotto is cooked, gently fold in the roasted butternut squash, chopped sage, Parmesan cheese, and butter. Stir until well combined and the butter is melted.
    - Season with salt and freshly ground black pepper to taste.
6. **Serve:**
    - Spoon the risotto onto plates or into bowls.
    - Garnish with additional Parmesan cheese and fresh sage if desired.

Enjoy your Butternut Squash and Sage Risotto—a creamy, comforting dish with a perfect balance of sweet and savory flavors!

Chicken and Leek Pie

Ingredients:

For the Filling:

- 2 tablespoons olive oil or unsalted butter
- 1 large onion, finely chopped
- 2-3 leeks, white and light green parts only, sliced and cleaned
- 2 cloves garlic, minced
- 2 cups cooked chicken, shredded or diced (use rotisserie chicken or poached chicken breasts/thighs)
- 1 cup frozen peas (or fresh peas, if available)
- 1 cup chicken or vegetable broth
- 1 cup whole milk or heavy cream
- 1/4 cup all-purpose flour
- 1 teaspoon dried thyme
- 1 teaspoon dried parsley (or 1 tablespoon fresh parsley, chopped)
- Salt and freshly ground black pepper, to taste

For the Pie Crust:

- 2 1/2 cups all-purpose flour
- 1 teaspoon salt
- 1 cup (2 sticks) unsalted butter, cold and cut into small cubes
- 1/4 to 1/2 cup ice water

Instructions:

1. **Prepare the Pie Crust:**
   - In a large bowl, combine the flour and salt.
   - Add the cold butter and use a pastry cutter or your fingers to work it into the flour until the mixture resembles coarse crumbs.
   - Gradually add ice water, a tablespoon at a time, until the dough just comes together. Avoid overworking the dough.
   - Divide the dough in half, shape each portion into a disk, and wrap in plastic wrap. Chill in the refrigerator for at least 30 minutes.
2. **Prepare the Filling:**
   - Heat olive oil or butter in a large skillet over medium heat.
   - Add the chopped onion and leeks. Cook until softened and lightly golden, about 8-10 minutes.
   - Add the minced garlic and cook for an additional minute.
   - Stir in the flour and cook for 2 minutes, allowing the flour to absorb the fat and lightly toast.

- Gradually whisk in the chicken broth and milk or cream, ensuring there are no lumps. Cook, stirring frequently, until the sauce thickens and becomes creamy.
- Stir in the cooked chicken, peas, dried thyme, dried parsley, salt, and pepper. Cook for an additional 5 minutes, then remove from heat and let cool slightly.

3. **Assemble the Pie:**
    - Preheat your oven to 375°F (190°C).
    - On a lightly floured surface, roll out one disk of dough to fit the bottom and sides of a 9-inch pie dish. Carefully transfer the dough to the pie dish, pressing it into the edges.
    - Pour the chicken and leek filling into the pie crust.
    - Roll out the second disk of dough and place it over the filling. Trim any excess dough and crimp the edges to seal the pie. Cut a few small slits in the top crust to allow steam to escape.

4. **Bake the Pie:**
    - Brush the top crust with a little milk or egg wash (beaten egg mixed with a tablespoon of water) for a golden finish.
    - Bake in the preheated oven for 35-40 minutes, or until the crust is golden brown and the filling is bubbling.

5. **Serve:**
    - Let the pie cool for about 10 minutes before serving to allow the filling to set.

Enjoy your Chicken and Leek Pie—a comforting and satisfying dish that's perfect for a cozy meal!

Veggie-stuffed Empanadas

Ingredients:

For the Dough:

- 2 1/2 cups all-purpose flour
- 1/2 teaspoon salt
- 1/2 cup unsalted butter, cold and cut into small cubes
- 1 large egg
- 1/4 cup cold water (more if needed)

For the Filling:

- 2 tablespoons olive oil
- 1 small onion, finely chopped
- 1 bell pepper (any color), diced
- 1 small zucchini, diced
- 1 cup frozen corn (or fresh corn)
- 1 cup spinach or kale, chopped
- 2 cloves garlic, minced
- 1 teaspoon ground cumin
- 1/2 teaspoon smoked paprika
- 1/2 teaspoon dried oregano
- Salt and freshly ground black pepper, to taste
- 1/2 cup shredded cheese (cheddar, Monterey Jack, or your choice, optional)

For Assembly:

- 1 egg, beaten (for egg wash)
- Optional: sesame seeds or poppy seeds for sprinkling

Instructions:

1. **Prepare the Dough:**
    - In a large bowl, combine the flour and salt.
    - Cut in the cold butter using a pastry cutter or your fingers until the mixture resembles coarse crumbs.
    - In a small bowl, whisk together the egg and cold water.
    - Gradually add the egg mixture to the flour mixture, stirring until the dough just comes together. You may need to add a little more water if the dough is too dry.
    - Turn the dough out onto a lightly floured surface and knead briefly until smooth.
    - Divide the dough in half, shape each portion into a disk, and wrap in plastic wrap. Chill in the refrigerator for at least 30 minutes.

2. **Prepare the Filling:**
   - Heat olive oil in a large skillet over medium heat.
   - Add the chopped onion and bell pepper, and cook until softened, about 5 minutes.
   - Add the zucchini, corn, and garlic. Cook for an additional 5 minutes.
   - Stir in the spinach or kale and cook until wilted.
   - Season the mixture with cumin, smoked paprika, oregano, salt, and pepper.
   - Remove from heat and let cool slightly. If using cheese, stir it in now.
3. **Assemble the Empanadas:**
   - Preheat your oven to 375°F (190°C).
   - On a lightly floured surface, roll out one disk of dough to about 1/8-inch thickness.
   - Use a round cutter or a glass to cut out circles of dough, about 4-5 inches in diameter.
   - Place a spoonful of filling in the center of each dough circle.
   - Fold the dough over to create a half-moon shape, and press the edges together to seal. You can crimp the edges with a fork or fold them over with your fingers.
   - Place the empanadas on a baking sheet lined with parchment paper.
   - Brush the tops with beaten egg and sprinkle with sesame seeds or poppy seeds if desired.
4. **Bake the Empanadas:**
   - Bake in the preheated oven for 20-25 minutes, or until the empanadas are golden brown and crisp.
5. **Serve:**
   - Let the empanadas cool slightly before serving. They can be enjoyed warm or at room temperature.

Enjoy your Veggie-Stuffed Empanadas—perfect for a party, lunch, or a satisfying snack!

Roast Beef and Horseradish Sandwich

Ingredients:

For the Sandwich:

- 1 pound thinly sliced roast beef (preferably from the deli or homemade)
- 4 slices of crusty bread (such as ciabatta, sourdough, or a baguette)
- 4 tablespoons horseradish sauce (adjust to taste, see recipe below)
- 4 tablespoons mayonnaise
- 1 cup arugula or baby spinach
- 1 small red onion, thinly sliced
- 4 slices of Swiss cheese or cheddar cheese (optional)
- Salt and freshly ground black pepper, to taste

For the Horseradish Sauce:

- 2 tablespoons prepared horseradish (store-bought or homemade)
- 1/2 cup sour cream
- 1 tablespoon Dijon mustard
- 1 teaspoon lemon juice
- Salt and freshly ground black pepper, to taste

Instructions:

1. **Prepare the Horseradish Sauce:**
    - In a small bowl, combine the prepared horseradish, sour cream, Dijon mustard, and lemon juice.
    - Mix well until smooth and season with salt and pepper to taste.
    - Adjust the level of horseradish to your preference for spiciness. Set aside.
2. **Assemble the Sandwich:**
    - Toast the bread slices lightly if desired for extra crunch.
    - Spread 1 tablespoon of horseradish sauce on each slice of bread.
    - Spread 1 tablespoon of mayonnaise on top of the horseradish sauce on each slice.
    - Layer slices of roast beef evenly over the mayo side of two of the bread slices.
    - Top the roast beef with Swiss cheese or cheddar cheese slices if using.
    - Add a handful of arugula or baby spinach on top of the roast beef.
    - Place the thinly sliced red onion on top of the greens.
    - Season with a little salt and pepper.
3. **Finish the Sandwich:**
    - Place the remaining slices of bread, mayo side down, on top of the prepared sandwiches.
    - If desired, cut the sandwiches in half for easier serving.

4. **Serve:**
    - Serve the sandwiches immediately. They are great with a side of pickles or chips.

Enjoy your Roast Beef and Horseradish Sandwich—a satisfying and flavorful meal with a perfect balance of rich and spicy flavors!

Atlantic Salmon Salad

Ingredients:

For the Salad:

- 2 (6-ounce) salmon fillets
- 1 tablespoon olive oil
- Salt and freshly ground black pepper, to taste
- 1 teaspoon dried dill or 1 tablespoon fresh dill (optional)
- 4 cups mixed greens (such as arugula, spinach, or baby kale)
- 1 cup cherry tomatoes, halved
- 1/2 cucumber, sliced
- 1/4 red onion, thinly sliced
- 1/2 avocado, sliced
- 1/4 cup crumbled feta cheese (optional)
- 1/4 cup black olives or Kalamata olives (optional)

For the Dressing:

- 3 tablespoons olive oil
- 1 tablespoon lemon juice
- 1 tablespoon Dijon mustard
- 1 teaspoon honey or maple syrup
- 1 garlic clove, minced
- Salt and freshly ground black pepper, to taste

Instructions:

1. **Prepare the Salmon:**
    - Preheat your oven to 375°F (190°C).
    - Place the salmon fillets on a baking sheet lined with parchment paper or lightly greased.
    - Rub the salmon with olive oil and season with salt, pepper, and dill (if using).
    - Bake for 15-20 minutes, or until the salmon is cooked through and flakes easily with a fork. Cooking time may vary depending on the thickness of the fillets. Let the salmon cool slightly.
2. **Prepare the Salad:**
    - In a large salad bowl, combine the mixed greens, cherry tomatoes, cucumber, red onion, and avocado.
    - If using, add crumbled feta cheese and black olives or Kalamata olives.
3. **Prepare the Dressing:**
    - In a small bowl or jar, whisk together the olive oil, lemon juice, Dijon mustard, honey or maple syrup, minced garlic, salt, and pepper until well combined.

4. **Assemble the Salad:**
    - Flake the cooled salmon into bite-sized pieces and place it on top of the salad.
    - Drizzle with the prepared dressing just before serving.
    - Gently toss the salad to combine, or serve the dressing on the side.
5. **Serve:**
    - Serve the salad immediately, or chill it in the refrigerator for up to an hour before serving.

Enjoy your Atlantic Salmon Salad—a light yet satisfying meal that pairs the rich flavor of salmon with fresh vegetables and a tangy dressing!

Stuffed Cornish Hen

Ingredients:

For the Cornish Hen:

- 4 Cornish hens (about 1 to 1.5 pounds each), thawed if frozen
- 2 tablespoons olive oil
- Salt and freshly ground black pepper, to taste
- 1 teaspoon dried thyme or rosemary (optional)
- 1 lemon, cut into wedges (optional, for roasting)

For the Stuffing:

- 2 tablespoons olive oil or unsalted butter
- 1 small onion, finely chopped
- 2 cloves garlic, minced
- 2 celery stalks, diced
- 1 cup diced carrots
- 2 cups stale bread cubes (white, whole wheat, or sourdough)
- 1/2 cup chicken or vegetable broth
- 1/4 cup fresh parsley, chopped
- 1 teaspoon dried sage
- 1/2 teaspoon dried thyme
- 1/4 teaspoon ground nutmeg
- Salt and freshly ground black pepper, to taste
- 1/4 cup grated Parmesan cheese (optional)

Instructions:

1. **Prepare the Stuffing:**
    - In a large skillet, heat olive oil or butter over medium heat.
    - Add the chopped onion, garlic, celery, and carrots. Cook until the vegetables are softened, about 5-7 minutes.
    - Add the bread cubes to the skillet and stir to combine.
    - Pour in the chicken or vegetable broth and stir until the bread is slightly softened.
    - Add the parsley, sage, thyme, nutmeg, salt, pepper, and Parmesan cheese (if using). Mix well and cook for another 2-3 minutes.
    - Remove from heat and let the stuffing cool slightly.
2. **Prepare the Cornish Hens:**
    - Preheat your oven to 375°F (190°C).
    - Rinse the Cornish hens and pat them dry with paper towels.
    - Rub the hens inside and out with olive oil, salt, pepper, and dried thyme or rosemary if desired.

- Stuff each hen with the prepared stuffing, packing it lightly. Secure the openings with toothpicks or tie the legs together with kitchen twine.
3. **Roast the Cornish Hens:**
    - Place the stuffed Cornish hens on a roasting pan or a rimmed baking sheet.
    - Optionally, place lemon wedges around the hens for added flavor.
    - Roast in the preheated oven for 50-60 minutes, or until the hens are golden brown and the internal temperature reaches 165°F (74°C) when measured at the thickest part of the thigh.
    - Baste the hens occasionally with the pan juices for a more even browning.
4. **Serve:**
    - Let the stuffed Cornish hens rest for about 10 minutes before carving.
    - Serve with additional stuffing on the side if desired, along with your favorite vegetables or a light salad.

Enjoy your Stuffed Cornish Hen—a perfect choice for a special occasion or a sophisticated family dinner!

Canadian Club Sandwich

Ingredients:

For the Sandwich:

- 3 slices of bread (white, whole wheat, or your choice)
- 2 tablespoons mayonnaise
- 2 tablespoons Dijon mustard (optional)
- 4 slices of cooked bacon
- 4 slices of roast turkey or chicken breast
- 2 slices of cheddar cheese (or your favorite cheese)
- 2-3 leaves of romaine lettuce or iceberg lettuce
- 2-3 slices of tomato
- Salt and freshly ground black pepper, to taste

Instructions:

1. **Prepare the Bread:**
   - Toast the bread slices until golden brown and crispy. Set aside.
2. **Assemble the Sandwich:**
   - Spread mayonnaise on one side of each slice of toasted bread. If using, spread Dijon mustard on one or two of the slices as well.
   - On the first slice of bread, layer 2 slices of roast turkey, 2 slices of cheddar cheese, and 2 slices of cooked bacon.
   - Top with a layer of lettuce and tomato slices.
   - Season the tomato with a little salt and pepper if desired.
   - Place the second slice of bread, mayonnaise side down, on top of the filling.
   - Repeat the layers with the remaining roast turkey, bacon, cheese, lettuce, and tomato.
   - Top with the third slice of bread, mayonnaise side down.
3. **Cut and Serve:**
   - If desired, cut the sandwich into quarters or halves for easier eating and to make it look more appealing.
   - Serve immediately with your favorite sides, such as potato chips, pickles, or a side salad.

Enjoy your Canadian Club Sandwich—a satisfying and classic choice for a tasty meal!

Tomato and Basil Bruschetta

Ingredients:

For the Bruschetta:

- 1 baguette or loaf of Italian bread
- 3-4 ripe tomatoes, finely diced
- 1/4 cup fresh basil leaves, chopped
- 2 cloves garlic, minced
- 2 tablespoons extra-virgin olive oil
- 1 tablespoon balsamic vinegar (optional)
- Salt and freshly ground black pepper, to taste

Instructions:

1. **Prepare the Tomato Mixture:**
    - In a medium bowl, combine the diced tomatoes, chopped basil, minced garlic, olive oil, and balsamic vinegar (if using).
    - Season with salt and pepper to taste. Mix well and let the mixture sit for about 10-15 minutes to allow the flavors to meld.
2. **Prepare the Bread:**
    - Preheat your oven to 400°F (200°C) or set a grill to medium-high heat.
    - Slice the baguette or Italian bread into 1/2-inch thick slices.
    - Arrange the slices on a baking sheet or grill rack.
    - Toast the bread in the oven for about 5-7 minutes or on the grill for 1-2 minutes per side, until golden and crisp. Watch closely to avoid burning.
3. **Assemble the Bruschetta:**
    - Once the bread is toasted, remove it from the oven or grill.
    - Spoon the tomato and basil mixture generously onto each slice of toasted bread.
4. **Serve:**
    - Serve the bruschetta immediately while the bread is still warm and crispy.

Optional Garnish:

- Drizzle with a bit more extra-virgin olive oil or balsamic glaze before serving.
- Top with a sprinkle of grated Parmesan cheese or a few extra basil leaves for a touch of elegance.

Enjoy your Tomato and Basil Bruschetta—a fresh, flavorful appetizer that's perfect for any occasion!

Potato and Chive Fritters

Ingredients:

- 4 medium potatoes (about 1 pound), peeled and grated
- 1 small onion, finely chopped
- 2 cloves garlic, minced
- 1/4 cup fresh chives, chopped
- 1/4 cup all-purpose flour
- 1 large egg
- Salt and freshly ground black pepper, to taste
- 1/2 teaspoon baking powder (optional, for extra crispiness)
- Vegetable oil for frying

Instructions:

1. **Prepare the Potatoes:**
    - Place the grated potatoes in a clean kitchen towel or cheesecloth and squeeze out as much excess moisture as possible. This step is crucial for crispy fritters.
2. **Mix the Ingredients:**
    - In a large bowl, combine the grated potatoes, chopped onion, minced garlic, chopped chives, flour, and egg. Mix well until everything is evenly incorporated.
    - Season with salt and pepper. Add baking powder if using, and mix again.
3. **Heat the Oil:**
    - Heat a generous amount of vegetable oil (about 1/4 inch deep) in a large skillet over medium heat. The oil should be hot but not smoking.
4. **Form and Fry the Fritters:**
    - Scoop about 2-3 tablespoons of the potato mixture and form it into a patty. Flatten it slightly with the back of the spoon or your hands.
    - Carefully place the patty in the hot oil. Repeat with remaining mixture, making sure not to overcrowd the skillet.
    - Fry for about 3-4 minutes per side, or until the fritters are golden brown and crispy. Adjust the heat as needed to prevent burning.
5. **Drain and Serve:**
    - Remove the fritters from the skillet and place them on a plate lined with paper towels to drain any excess oil.
    - Serve warm. These fritters are delicious on their own or with a side of sour cream, applesauce, or your favorite dipping sauce.

Enjoy your Potato and Chive Fritters—a tasty and versatile dish that's sure to be a hit!

Teriyaki Chicken Skewers

Ingredients:

For the Marinade:

- 1/2 cup soy sauce
- 1/4 cup honey or brown sugar
- 1/4 cup rice vinegar or apple cider vinegar
- 2 tablespoons mirin (optional)
- 2 tablespoons sesame oil
- 2 cloves garlic, minced
- 1 tablespoon fresh ginger, minced
- 1 tablespoon cornstarch mixed with 2 tablespoons water (to thicken)

For the Chicken Skewers:

- 1 1/2 pounds boneless, skinless chicken breasts or thighs, cut into bite-sized pieces
- Wooden or metal skewers (if using wooden skewers, soak them in water for at least 30 minutes before using)

Instructions:

1. **Prepare the Marinade:**
   - In a bowl, whisk together the soy sauce, honey (or brown sugar), rice vinegar, mirin (if using), sesame oil, minced garlic, and minced ginger.
   - Stir in the cornstarch mixture to thicken the marinade slightly.
2. **Marinate the Chicken:**
   - Place the chicken pieces in a large resealable plastic bag or a shallow dish.
   - Pour half of the marinade over the chicken and toss to coat. Reserve the remaining marinade for basting.
   - Seal the bag or cover the dish and refrigerate for at least 30 minutes, or up to 2 hours for more flavor.
3. **Prepare the Skewers:**
   - Preheat your grill to medium-high heat, or preheat your oven's broiler.
   - Thread the marinated chicken pieces onto the skewers, leaving a little space between each piece.
4. **Cook the Skewers:**
   - **For Grilling:**
     - Brush the grill grates with oil to prevent sticking.
     - Grill the skewers for about 3-4 minutes per side, or until the chicken is cooked through and has nice grill marks. Baste occasionally with the reserved marinade.
   - **For Broiling:**

- Place the skewers on a broiler pan or a rack set over a baking sheet.
- Broil the skewers about 4-6 inches from the heat source for 4-5 minutes per side, or until the chicken is cooked through and slightly charred. Baste occasionally with the reserved marinade.

5. **Serve:**
    - Remove the skewers from the grill or oven and let them rest for a few minutes.
    - Serve the Teriyaki Chicken Skewers with steamed rice, sautéed vegetables, or a side salad.

Enjoy your Teriyaki Chicken Skewers—an easy and flavorful dish that's perfect for any occasion!

Crab Cakes with Lemon Aioli

Ingredients:

For the Crab Cakes:

- 1 pound fresh crab meat (lump or claw meat, picked over for shells)
- 1/2 cup mayonnaise
- 1 large egg
- 1 tablespoon Dijon mustard
- 1 tablespoon Worcestershire sauce
- 1 teaspoon Old Bay seasoning (or your favorite seafood seasoning)
- 1/4 cup finely chopped fresh parsley
- 1/4 cup finely chopped green onions (scallions)
- 1/4 cup finely diced red bell pepper (optional, for color)
- 1 cup panko breadcrumbs (plus extra for coating)
- Salt and freshly ground black pepper, to taste
- 2 tablespoons olive oil or vegetable oil (for frying)

For the Lemon Aioli:

- 1/2 cup mayonnaise
- 1 tablespoon lemon juice
- 1 teaspoon lemon zest
- 1 clove garlic, minced
- 1 teaspoon Dijon mustard
- Salt and freshly ground black pepper, to taste

Instructions:

1. **Prepare the Crab Cakes:**
    - In a large bowl, combine the mayonnaise, egg, Dijon mustard, Worcestershire sauce, Old Bay seasoning, chopped parsley, green onions, and diced red bell pepper (if using).
    - Gently fold in the crab meat, being careful not to break up the lumps too much.
    - Gradually add the panko breadcrumbs, mixing until the mixture holds together but isn't too dry. You may need a bit more or less breadcrumbs depending on the moisture of the crab meat.
    - Season with salt and pepper to taste.
    - Form the mixture into 8-10 patties, about 1/2 to 3/4 inch thick. Coat each patty lightly with additional panko breadcrumbs for extra crispiness.
2. **Prepare the Lemon Aioli:**
    - In a small bowl, whisk together the mayonnaise, lemon juice, lemon zest, minced garlic, and Dijon mustard.

- Season with salt and pepper to taste. Adjust the lemon juice and garlic to your preference.
- Cover and refrigerate until ready to serve.

3. **Cook the Crab Cakes:**
    - Heat the olive oil or vegetable oil in a large skillet over medium heat.
    - Fry the crab cakes in batches, being careful not to overcrowd the pan. Cook for 3-4 minutes per side, or until golden brown and crisp.
    - Transfer the cooked crab cakes to a plate lined with paper towels to drain any excess oil.
4. **Serve:**
    - Serve the crab cakes warm with a side of lemon aioli.
    - Garnish with additional chopped parsley or lemon wedges if desired.

Enjoy your Crab Cakes with Lemon Aioli—tender, flavorful crab cakes paired with a tangy and creamy dipping sauce for a delicious treat!

Shepherd's Pie

Ingredients:

For the Meat Filling:

- 1 tablespoon olive oil
- 1 large onion, finely chopped
- 2 cloves garlic, minced
- 1 large carrot, diced
- 1 cup frozen peas
- 1 cup frozen corn (optional)
- 1 pound ground lamb or beef (or a mixture of both)
- 2 tablespoons tomato paste
- 1 tablespoon Worcestershire sauce
- 1 cup beef or chicken broth
- 1 teaspoon dried thyme
- 1 teaspoon dried rosemary
- Salt and freshly ground black pepper, to taste

For the Mashed Potatoes:

- 4 large potatoes, peeled and cubed
- 1/2 cup milk (or cream for a richer texture)
- 1/4 cup unsalted butter
- Salt and freshly ground black pepper, to taste
- 1/4 cup grated cheddar cheese (optional, for extra flavor)

Instructions:

1. **Prepare the Mashed Potatoes:**
    - Place the peeled and cubed potatoes in a large pot and cover with cold water.
    - Bring to a boil and cook for 15-20 minutes, or until the potatoes are tender when pierced with a fork.
    - Drain the potatoes and return them to the pot.
    - Add the milk and butter to the potatoes. Mash until smooth and creamy. Season with salt and pepper to taste.
    - Stir in the grated cheddar cheese if using. Set aside.
2. **Prepare the Meat Filling:**
    - Heat olive oil in a large skillet or saucepan over medium heat.
    - Add the chopped onion and cook until softened, about 5 minutes.
    - Add the minced garlic and diced carrot. Cook for another 5 minutes.
    - Add the ground lamb or beef to the skillet and cook until browned and cooked through. Break up the meat with a spoon as it cooks.

- Stir in the tomato paste and Worcestershire sauce. Cook for 2 minutes.
- Add the beef or chicken broth, frozen peas, and corn (if using). Stir well.
- Sprinkle in the dried thyme and rosemary. Season with salt and pepper.
- Simmer the mixture for about 5 minutes, until the vegetables are tender and the filling has thickened slightly.

3. **Assemble the Shepherd's Pie:**
    - Preheat your oven to 400°F (200°C).
    - Transfer the meat filling to a baking dish (about 8x8 inches or similar).
    - Spread the mashed potatoes evenly over the meat filling. Use a fork to create a textured pattern on the surface of the potatoes, which helps them brown nicely.
    - Optional: Sprinkle a little extra cheese on top for a golden, cheesy crust.

4. **Bake the Shepherd's Pie:**
    - Bake in the preheated oven for 20-25 minutes, or until the top is golden brown and the filling is bubbling around the edges.

5. **Serve:**
    - Let the Shepherd's Pie cool for a few minutes before serving.

Enjoy your Shepherd's Pie—a hearty, comforting meal with a flavorful meat filling and a creamy mashed potato topping!

BBQ Chicken Quesadilla

Ingredients:

- 2 cups cooked chicken, shredded or diced (such as rotisserie chicken or leftover grilled chicken)
- 1/2 cup BBQ sauce (your favorite brand or homemade)
- 1 tablespoon olive oil
- 4 large flour tortillas
- 1 1/2 cups shredded cheddar cheese (or a blend of cheddar and Monterey Jack)
- 1/2 cup red onion, thinly sliced
- 1/2 cup sliced bell peppers (any color)
- 1/2 cup corn kernels (optional)
- 1/4 cup chopped fresh cilantro (optional, for garnish)
- Sour cream and salsa (for serving, optional)

Instructions:

1. **Prepare the BBQ Chicken:**
    - In a bowl, combine the shredded or diced chicken with the BBQ sauce. Mix until the chicken is well coated. Set aside.
2. **Prepare the Vegetables:**
    - If using, heat the olive oil in a skillet over medium heat.
    - Add the sliced red onion and bell peppers. Sauté for 5-7 minutes until they are tender and slightly caramelized.
    - If using corn, add it to the skillet and cook for an additional 1-2 minutes. Remove from heat and set aside.
3. **Assemble the Quesadillas:**
    - Place one tortilla in a large skillet or on a griddle over medium heat.
    - Sprinkle half of the shredded cheese evenly over the tortilla.
    - Spoon half of the BBQ chicken mixture over the cheese.
    - Add half of the sautéed vegetables and sprinkle with a little more cheese if desired. This extra cheese helps to bind the quesadilla together.
    - Top with another tortilla.
4. **Cook the Quesadilla:**
    - Cook the quesadilla for 2-3 minutes on one side, or until the tortilla is golden brown and crispy. Carefully flip it over and cook for another 2-3 minutes on the other side, until the cheese is melted and the tortilla is crispy.
    - Remove from the skillet and let it cool for a minute before cutting.
5. **Serve:**
    - Cut the quesadilla into wedges and serve with sour cream, salsa, or any additional toppings you like.
    - Garnish with chopped fresh cilantro if desired.

Enjoy your BBQ Chicken Quesadilla—crispy, cheesy, and packed with delicious BBQ flavor!

Beet and Goat Cheese Salad

Ingredients:

For the Salad:

- 4 medium beets (red or golden, or a mix)
- 4 cups mixed greens (such as arugula, spinach, or baby kale)
- 4 ounces goat cheese, crumbled
- 1/4 cup toasted walnuts or pecans (optional)
- 1/4 cup thinly sliced red onion (optional)
- 1/4 cup fresh herbs (such as parsley or dill), chopped (optional)

For the Vinaigrette:

- 3 tablespoons extra-virgin olive oil
- 1 tablespoon balsamic vinegar or red wine vinegar
- 1 teaspoon Dijon mustard
- 1 teaspoon honey or maple syrup
- Salt and freshly ground black pepper, to taste

Instructions:

1. **Prepare the Beets:**
    - Preheat your oven to 400°F (200°C).
    - Wash the beets and trim off the greens (save the greens if you want to use them in another dish).
    - Wrap each beet in aluminum foil and place them on a baking sheet.
    - Roast in the preheated oven for 45-60 minutes, or until the beets are tender when pierced with a fork. Cooking time will depend on the size of the beets.
    - Let the beets cool slightly, then peel them (the skin should come off easily) and cut them into wedges or slices.
2. **Prepare the Vinaigrette:**
    - In a small bowl or jar, whisk together the olive oil, balsamic vinegar, Dijon mustard, honey or maple syrup, salt, and pepper until well combined.
3. **Assemble the Salad:**
    - In a large salad bowl, toss the mixed greens with a little bit of the vinaigrette.
    - Arrange the roasted beet slices on top of the greens.
    - Sprinkle crumbled goat cheese over the beets.
    - Add the toasted walnuts or pecans, and thinly sliced red onion if using.
    - Garnish with fresh herbs if desired.
4. **Serve:**
    - Drizzle the remaining vinaigrette over the salad just before serving, or serve it on the side.

    - Serve immediately or chill in the refrigerator for a short period before serving.

Enjoy your Beet and Goat Cheese Salad—a delicious and colorful salad that combines sweet, tangy, and earthy flavors!

Lamb and Mint Burgers

Ingredients:

- 1 pound ground lamb
- 1/4 cup fresh mint leaves, finely chopped
- 2 cloves garlic, minced
- 1 teaspoon ground cumin
- 1 teaspoon ground coriander
- 1/2 teaspoon smoked paprika
- 1/2 teaspoon ground black pepper
- 1/2 teaspoon salt
- 1 egg, lightly beaten (optional, for binding)
- 1/4 cup breadcrumbs (optional, for binding)

For Serving:

- Burger buns
- Lettuce leaves
- Tomato slices
- Red onion slices
- Cucumber slices
- Tzatziki sauce or yogurt-based sauce (optional)
- Feta cheese (optional)

Instructions:

1. **Prepare the Burger Mixture:**
    - In a large bowl, combine the ground lamb, chopped mint, minced garlic, ground cumin, ground coriander, smoked paprika, black pepper, and salt.
    - If using, add the beaten egg and breadcrumbs to help bind the mixture together. Mix until all ingredients are well combined, but avoid over-mixing to keep the burgers tender.
2. **Form the Patties:**
    - Divide the mixture into 4 equal portions and shape them into patties, about 3/4 inch thick. Press a small dimple in the center of each patty to help them cook evenly and maintain their shape.
3. **Cook the Burgers:**
    - **Grilling:** Preheat your grill to medium-high heat. Lightly oil the grill grates. Grill the patties for 4-5 minutes per side, or until they reach an internal temperature of 160°F (71°C) for medium doneness. Adjust cooking time as needed for your desired level of doneness.

- **Pan-Frying:** Heat a little oil in a large skillet over medium-high heat. Cook the patties for 4-5 minutes per side, or until they reach an internal temperature of 160°F (71°C) for medium doneness.

4. **Assemble the Burgers:**
   - Toast the burger buns lightly, if desired.
   - Place a lamb patty on each bun and top with your choice of lettuce, tomato slices, red onion slices, and cucumber slices.
   - Add a dollop of tzatziki sauce or yogurt-based sauce on top of the patties if desired, and sprinkle with feta cheese if using.
5. **Serve:**
   - Serve the Lamb and Mint Burgers immediately with your favorite side dishes, such as roasted vegetables, potato wedges, or a fresh salad.

Enjoy your Lamb and Mint Burgers—a flavorful and unique take on the classic burger that's sure to impress!

Ginger Beef Stir-Fry

Ingredients:

For the Stir-Fry:

- 1 pound flank steak or sirloin, thinly sliced against the grain
- 2 tablespoons vegetable oil (or another high-heat oil)
- 1 red bell pepper, sliced
- 1 yellow bell pepper, sliced
- 1 cup snap peas or snow peas
- 1 cup broccoli florets
- 1 medium carrot, thinly sliced or julienned
- 3 green onions, sliced
- 2 cloves garlic, minced
- 1 tablespoon fresh ginger, minced

For the Sauce:

- 1/4 cup soy sauce
- 2 tablespoons hoisin sauce
- 1 tablespoon oyster sauce (optional)
- 1 tablespoon rice vinegar or apple cider vinegar
- 1 tablespoon brown sugar or honey
- 1 teaspoon cornstarch mixed with 2 tablespoons water (for thickening)
- 1/2 teaspoon sesame oil (optional, for added flavor)

Instructions:

1. **Prepare the Sauce:**
   - In a small bowl, whisk together the soy sauce, hoisin sauce, oyster sauce (if using), rice vinegar, and brown sugar or honey.
   - Stir in the cornstarch-water mixture. This will help thicken the sauce when it's cooked.
   - Set aside.
2. **Cook the Beef:**
   - Heat 1 tablespoon of vegetable oil in a large skillet or wok over medium-high heat.
   - Add the thinly sliced beef in a single layer and cook for 2-3 minutes, or until browned. Avoid overcrowding the pan; you may need to cook the beef in batches.
   - Remove the beef from the skillet and set aside.
3. **Stir-Fry the Vegetables:**
   - In the same skillet, add the remaining 1 tablespoon of vegetable oil.

- - Add the sliced bell peppers, snap peas, broccoli florets, and carrots. Stir-fry for 3-4 minutes, or until the vegetables are crisp-tender.
  - Add the minced garlic and ginger, and cook for an additional 1 minute until fragrant.
4. **Combine and Finish:**
    - Return the cooked beef to the skillet with the vegetables.
    - Pour the prepared sauce over the beef and vegetables.
    - Stir well to combine and cook for another 2-3 minutes, or until the sauce has thickened and everything is heated through.
5. **Serve:**
    - Garnish with sliced green onions and a drizzle of sesame oil if desired.
    - Serve the Ginger Beef Stir-Fry over steamed rice, noodles, or on its own.

Enjoy your Ginger Beef Stir-Fry—quick, easy, and packed with delicious flavors!

Spinach and Feta Stuffed Chicken

Ingredients:

- 4 boneless, skinless chicken breasts
- 1 tablespoon olive oil
- 2 cups fresh spinach, chopped
- 1/2 cup crumbled feta cheese
- 1/4 cup grated Parmesan cheese
- 2 cloves garlic, minced
- 1/4 teaspoon dried oregano
- 1/4 teaspoon dried thyme
- Salt and freshly ground black pepper, to taste
- Toothpicks or kitchen twine (for securing the chicken)

For the Basting:

- 1 tablespoon olive oil
- 1/2 teaspoon dried oregano
- 1/2 teaspoon garlic powder
- Salt and freshly ground black pepper, to taste

Instructions:

1. **Prepare the Filling:**
    - In a medium skillet, heat 1 tablespoon of olive oil over medium heat.
    - Add the minced garlic and cook for about 1 minute, until fragrant.
    - Add the chopped spinach and cook for 2-3 minutes, until wilted and most of the moisture has evaporated.
    - Remove from heat and let cool slightly.
    - In a bowl, combine the cooked spinach, crumbled feta cheese, grated Parmesan cheese, dried oregano, and dried thyme. Season with salt and pepper to taste.
2. **Prepare the Chicken:**
    - Preheat your oven to 375°F (190°C).
    - Place each chicken breast between two sheets of plastic wrap or parchment paper.
    - Using a meat mallet or rolling pin, gently pound the chicken breasts to an even thickness (about 1/2 inch thick).
    - Carefully cut a pocket into each chicken breast by slicing horizontally but not all the way through.
3. **Stuff the Chicken:**
    - Spoon the spinach and feta mixture into the pocket of each chicken breast.

- Use toothpicks or kitchen twine to secure the opening of each chicken breast, ensuring the filling stays inside during cooking.

4. **Season and Cook:**
   - In a small bowl, mix together 1 tablespoon of olive oil, dried oregano, garlic powder, salt, and pepper.
   - Brush or rub the seasoning mixture over each stuffed chicken breast.
   - Heat a large oven-safe skillet over medium-high heat and add a little olive oil.
   - Sear the chicken breasts for 2-3 minutes on each side, until golden brown.

5. **Bake the Chicken:**
   - Transfer the skillet to the preheated oven.
   - Bake for 20-25 minutes, or until the chicken is cooked through and reaches an internal temperature of 165°F (74°C).
   - Remove from the oven and let the chicken rest for a few minutes before removing the toothpicks or twine.

6. **Serve:**
   - Slice the stuffed chicken breasts if desired and serve with your favorite side dishes, such as roasted vegetables, rice, or a fresh salad.

Enjoy your Spinach and Feta Stuffed Chicken—tender, juicy chicken with a flavorful and creamy filling!

Blackened Tilapia Tacos

Ingredients:

For the Blackened Tilapia:

- 4 tilapia fillets (about 6 ounces each)
- 2 tablespoons olive oil
- 1 tablespoon paprika
- 1 teaspoon cayenne pepper (adjust to taste for heat)
- 1 teaspoon onion powder
- 1 teaspoon garlic powder
- 1 teaspoon dried thyme
- 1 teaspoon dried oregano
- 1/2 teaspoon ground black pepper
- 1/2 teaspoon salt

For the Tacos:

- 8 small tortillas (corn or flour, your preference)
- 1 cup shredded cabbage or coleslaw mix
- 1/2 cup diced tomatoes
- 1/4 cup finely chopped red onion
- 1/4 cup chopped fresh cilantro
- 1 avocado, sliced
- Lime wedges (for serving)

For the Lime Crema (optional):

- 1/2 cup sour cream or Greek yogurt
- 1 tablespoon lime juice
- 1 teaspoon lime zest
- 1 clove garlic, minced
- Salt and pepper to taste

Instructions:

1. **Prepare the Blackened Seasoning:**
   - In a small bowl, combine the paprika, cayenne pepper, onion powder, garlic powder, dried thyme, dried oregano, black pepper, and salt. Mix well.
2. **Season the Tilapia:**
   - Pat the tilapia fillets dry with paper towels.
   - Rub the tilapia fillets with olive oil on both sides.

- Generously coat the fillets with the blackened seasoning mixture, pressing it onto the fish to adhere.
3. **Cook the Tilapia:**
    - Heat a large skillet over medium-high heat. Add a little olive oil if needed.
    - Once the skillet is hot, add the tilapia fillets.
    - Cook the tilapia for 3-4 minutes per side, or until the fish is cooked through and has a blackened crust. The fish should flake easily with a fork.
    - Remove the tilapia from the skillet and let it rest for a few minutes before breaking it into chunks.
4. **Prepare the Lime Crema (optional):**
    - In a small bowl, mix together the sour cream (or Greek yogurt), lime juice, lime zest, minced garlic, salt, and pepper until smooth.
    - Adjust seasoning to taste and refrigerate until ready to use.
5. **Assemble the Tacos:**
    - Warm the tortillas in a dry skillet or in the oven.
    - Spread a bit of the lime crema (if using) on each tortilla.
    - Top with shredded cabbage or coleslaw mix.
    - Add chunks of blackened tilapia on top of the cabbage.
    - Garnish with diced tomatoes, chopped red onion, avocado slices, and fresh cilantro.
6. **Serve:**
    - Serve the tacos with lime wedges for squeezing over the top.
    - Enjoy immediately!

These Blackened Tilapia Tacos are sure to be a hit with their flavorful fish, fresh toppings, and zesty crema!

Roasted Veggie and Hummus Wrap

Ingredients:

For the Roasted Vegetables:

- 1 red bell pepper, sliced
- 1 yellow bell pepper, sliced
- 1 medium zucchini, sliced
- 1 small red onion, sliced
- 1 cup cherry tomatoes, halved
- 2 tablespoons olive oil
- 1 teaspoon dried oregano
- 1 teaspoon dried basil
- 1/2 teaspoon garlic powder
- Salt and freshly ground black pepper, to taste

For the Wraps:

- 4 large whole wheat or flour tortillas
- 1 cup hummus (store-bought or homemade)
- 1 cup baby spinach or mixed greens
- 1/4 cup crumbled feta cheese (optional)
- 1/4 cup sliced black olives (optional)
- 1 avocado, sliced (optional)
- 1/4 cup fresh basil or cilantro, chopped (optional)

Instructions:

1. **Roast the Vegetables:**
    - Preheat your oven to 400°F (200°C).
    - On a large baking sheet, toss the sliced red bell pepper, yellow bell pepper, zucchini, red onion, and cherry tomatoes with olive oil, dried oregano, dried basil, garlic powder, salt, and pepper.
    - Spread the vegetables in an even layer on the baking sheet.
    - Roast in the preheated oven for 20-25 minutes, or until the vegetables are tender and slightly caramelized. Stir halfway through the cooking time for even roasting.
    - Remove from the oven and let cool slightly.
2. **Prepare the Wraps:**
    - Warm the tortillas in a dry skillet or microwave for a few seconds to make them more pliable.
    - Spread a generous layer of hummus over each tortilla.
    - Layer on the roasted vegetables.

- Top with baby spinach or mixed greens, crumbled feta cheese (if using), sliced black olives (if using), and avocado slices (if using).
- Garnish with fresh basil or cilantro, if desired.
3. **Wrap and Serve:**
- Roll up each tortilla tightly, folding in the sides as you go to create a wrap.
- Slice the wraps in half diagonally if desired.
- Serve immediately, or wrap in foil or plastic wrap to take with you for a portable lunch or snack.

These Roasted Veggie and Hummus Wraps are a versatile and satisfying meal that's both healthy and packed with flavor. Feel free to customize with your favorite veggies or add some extra protein like grilled chicken or chickpeas if you like!

Spicy Butternut Squash Soup

Ingredients:

- 1 large butternut squash, peeled, seeded, and cubed (about 4 cups)
- 1 tablespoon olive oil
- 1 large onion, chopped
- 2 cloves garlic, minced
- 1 tablespoon fresh ginger, minced (or 1 teaspoon ground ginger)
- 1-2 teaspoons ground cumin (adjust to taste)
- 1 teaspoon smoked paprika
- 1/2 teaspoon ground turmeric (optional, for color)
- 1/4 to 1/2 teaspoon cayenne pepper (adjust to taste for heat)
- 4 cups vegetable broth (or chicken broth)
- 1 can (14.5 ounces) diced tomatoes
- 1 can (14 ounces) coconut milk
- Salt and freshly ground black pepper, to taste
- Fresh cilantro or parsley, chopped (for garnish)
- Lime wedges (for serving, optional)

Instructions:

1. **Prepare the Butternut Squash:**
    - Preheat your oven to 400°F (200°C).
    - Toss the cubed butternut squash with a little olive oil, salt, and pepper.
    - Spread the squash on a baking sheet in a single layer.
    - Roast for 25-30 minutes, or until the squash is tender and caramelized. Stir halfway through for even roasting.
2. **Cook the Soup Base:**
    - In a large pot or Dutch oven, heat 1 tablespoon of olive oil over medium heat.
    - Add the chopped onion and cook for 5-7 minutes, until softened and translucent.
    - Add the minced garlic and ginger, and cook for another minute, until fragrant.
    - Stir in the cumin, smoked paprika, turmeric (if using), and cayenne pepper. Cook for 1 minute to toast the spices.
3. **Combine and Simmer:**
    - Add the roasted butternut squash, vegetable broth, and diced tomatoes to the pot.
    - Bring to a boil, then reduce the heat and simmer for 10 minutes to allow the flavors to meld.
4. **Blend the Soup:**
    - Using an immersion blender, blend the soup directly in the pot until smooth. Alternatively, you can blend the soup in batches using a regular blender, but be sure to let it cool slightly before blending.

        - Stir in the coconut milk and season with salt and freshly ground black pepper to taste.
        - Heat the soup gently until warmed through, but do not boil.
5. **Serve:**
        - Ladle the soup into bowls and garnish with chopped fresh cilantro or parsley.
        - Serve with lime wedges on the side for a touch of brightness, if desired.

Enjoy your Spicy Butternut Squash Soup—a creamy, spicy, and wonderfully comforting dish!

Pear and Gorgonzola Salad

Ingredients:

For the Salad:

- 6 cups mixed greens (such as baby spinach, arugula, and/or baby kale)
- 2 ripe pears, cored and sliced (such as Bosc or Bartlett)
- 1/2 cup crumbled Gorgonzola cheese
- 1/4 cup toasted walnuts or pecans
- 1/4 cup thinly sliced red onion (optional)
- 1/4 cup dried cranberries or pomegranate seeds (optional)
- Fresh herbs (such as mint or basil) for garnish (optional)

For the Vinaigrette:

- 3 tablespoons extra-virgin olive oil
- 1 tablespoon balsamic vinegar (or red wine vinegar)
- 1 teaspoon Dijon mustard
- 1 teaspoon honey or maple syrup
- Salt and freshly ground black pepper, to taste

Instructions:

1. **Prepare the Vinaigrette:**
    - In a small bowl or jar, whisk together the olive oil, balsamic vinegar, Dijon mustard, and honey or maple syrup.
    - Season with salt and pepper to taste. Whisk until well combined or shake in a jar until emulsified. Set aside.
2. **Prepare the Salad Ingredients:**
    - Wash and dry the mixed greens. Place them in a large salad bowl.
    - Core and slice the pears into thin wedges. If you prefer, you can toss the pear slices with a little lemon juice to prevent browning.
3. **Assemble the Salad:**
    - Arrange the sliced pears on top of the mixed greens.
    - Sprinkle the crumbled Gorgonzola cheese over the pears and greens.
    - Add the toasted walnuts or pecans, and thinly sliced red onion if using.
    - Sprinkle dried cranberries or pomegranate seeds on top, if desired.
    - Garnish with fresh herbs if you like.
4. **Dress the Salad:**
    - Just before serving, drizzle the prepared vinaigrette over the salad.
    - Gently toss to combine, making sure the greens and other ingredients are evenly coated with the dressing.
5. **Serve:**

- Serve the salad immediately for the best texture and flavor.

Enjoy your Pear and Gorgonzola Salad—an elegant and flavorful combination that's perfect for any occasion!

Chicken Pot Pie

Ingredients:

For the Filling:

- 2 cups cooked chicken, diced or shredded (about 2-3 boneless, skinless chicken breasts)
- 1 tablespoon olive oil or butter
- 1 medium onion, diced
- 2 cloves garlic, minced
- 2 medium carrots, diced
- 2 celery stalks, diced
- 1 cup frozen peas
- 1/2 cup frozen corn (optional)
- 1/4 cup all-purpose flour
- 1 1/2 cups chicken broth
- 1 cup milk or heavy cream
- 1 teaspoon dried thyme
- 1/2 teaspoon dried rosemary
- Salt and freshly ground black pepper, to taste

For the Pie Crust:

- 1 batch of pie dough (store-bought or homemade) for a double-crust pie
    - **Homemade Pie Dough Ingredients:**
        - 2 1/2 cups all-purpose flour
        - 1 teaspoon salt
        - 1 cup (2 sticks) unsalted butter, chilled and cut into small cubes
        - 1/4 to 1/2 cup ice water

Instructions:

1. **Prepare the Pie Dough (if making homemade):**
    - In a large bowl, whisk together the flour and salt.
    - Cut in the chilled butter using a pastry cutter or your fingers until the mixture resembles coarse crumbs.
    - Gradually add ice water, 1 tablespoon at a time, mixing until the dough comes together. Do not overwork the dough.
    - Divide the dough in half, shape into discs, wrap in plastic wrap, and refrigerate for at least 30 minutes.
2. **Prepare the Filling:**
    - In a large skillet or saucepan, heat the olive oil or butter over medium heat.
    - Add the diced onion and cook until softened, about 3-4 minutes.

- Add the minced garlic and cook for another 1 minute.
- Add the diced carrots and celery, and cook for about 5 minutes, until they start to soften.
- Stir in the flour and cook for 1-2 minutes to form a roux.
- Gradually whisk in the chicken broth and milk or cream, and cook until the mixture starts to thicken.
- Stir in the cooked chicken, frozen peas, and corn (if using).
- Season with dried thyme, dried rosemary, salt, and pepper.
- Remove from heat and set aside to cool slightly.

3. **Assemble the Pot Pie:**
    - Preheat your oven to 400°F (200°C).
    - Roll out one of the chilled pie dough discs on a lightly floured surface to fit your pie dish.
    - Transfer the dough to the pie dish and trim the edges.
    - Pour the chicken filling into the pie crust.
    - Roll out the second dough disc and place it over the filling. Trim and crimp the edges to seal.
    - Cut a few slits in the top crust to allow steam to escape.

4. **Bake the Pot Pie:**
    - Place the pie on a baking sheet to catch any drips.
    - Bake in the preheated oven for 30-40 minutes, or until the crust is golden brown and the filling is bubbly.
    - If the edges of the crust start to brown too quickly, cover them with aluminum foil.

5. **Cool and Serve:**
    - Allow the pot pie to cool for about 10 minutes before serving. This helps the filling set and makes it easier to cut.

Enjoy your Chicken Pot Pie—rich, creamy, and full of comforting flavors!

Maple Bacon Brussels Sprouts

Ingredients:

- 1 pound Brussels sprouts, trimmed and halved
- 6 slices bacon, chopped
- 2 tablespoons maple syrup
- 2 tablespoons olive oil
- 2 cloves garlic, minced
- Salt and freshly ground black pepper, to taste
- 1/4 cup chopped pecans or walnuts (optional, for added crunch)
- 1/4 teaspoon red pepper flakes (optional, for a bit of heat)
- Fresh parsley, chopped (for garnish, optional)

Instructions:

1. **Prepare the Brussels Sprouts:**
    - Trim the ends off the Brussels sprouts and cut them in half. If some are particularly large, you can cut them into quarters to ensure even cooking.
2. **Cook the Bacon:**
    - In a large skillet, cook the chopped bacon over medium heat until crispy and browned, about 5-7 minutes.
    - Use a slotted spoon to remove the bacon from the skillet and transfer it to a paper-towel-lined plate to drain. Leave the bacon drippings in the skillet.
3. **Cook the Brussels Sprouts:**
    - Add the olive oil to the skillet with the bacon drippings and heat over medium-high heat.
    - Add the halved Brussels sprouts to the skillet, cut side down. Let them cook undisturbed for about 4-5 minutes, or until they start to brown.
    - Stir the Brussels sprouts and cook for an additional 5-7 minutes, or until they are tender and caramelized.
4. **Add Garlic and Seasonings:**
    - Add the minced garlic to the skillet and cook for 1 minute, until fragrant.
    - Season with salt, black pepper, and red pepper flakes (if using).
5. **Finish the Dish:**
    - Stir in the maple syrup and cook for 1-2 minutes, allowing it to slightly caramelize and coat the Brussels sprouts.
    - Add the crispy bacon back to the skillet and toss to combine.
6. **Add Nuts and Garnish:**
    - If using, stir in the chopped pecans or walnuts for added crunch.
    - Garnish with freshly chopped parsley if desired.
7. **Serve:**
    - Transfer the Brussels sprouts to a serving dish and serve warm.

Enjoy your Maple Bacon Brussels Sprouts—a perfect balance of sweet, savory, and crunchy flavors!

Poutine with Pulled Pork

Ingredients:

For the Fries:

- 4 large russet potatoes, peeled and cut into fries
- 2 tablespoons vegetable oil
- Salt and freshly ground black pepper, to taste

For the Pulled Pork:

- 2 pounds pork shoulder or pork butt
- 1 tablespoon vegetable oil
- 1 large onion, chopped
- 2 cloves garlic, minced
- 1 cup barbecue sauce (store-bought or homemade)
- 1 cup chicken broth
- 1 tablespoon apple cider vinegar
- 1 tablespoon brown sugar (optional, for extra sweetness)
- Salt and freshly ground black pepper, to taste

For the Gravy:

- 2 tablespoons unsalted butter
- 2 tablespoons all-purpose flour
- 2 cups beef or chicken broth
- Salt and freshly ground black pepper, to taste

For Assembly:

- 1 cup cheese curds (or shredded mozzarella if cheese curds are not available)
- Fresh parsley, chopped (for garnish, optional)

Instructions:

1. **Prepare the Pulled Pork:**
   - Season the pork shoulder with salt and pepper.
   - Heat the vegetable oil in a large skillet or Dutch oven over medium-high heat.
   - Sear the pork shoulder on all sides until browned, about 4-5 minutes per side.
   - Transfer the pork to a slow cooker.
   - In the same skillet, add the chopped onion and cook until softened, about 5 minutes. Add the minced garlic and cook for an additional 1 minute.

- Pour the barbecue sauce, chicken broth, apple cider vinegar, and brown sugar (if using) over the pork in the slow cooker.
- Cover and cook on low for 8 hours, or until the pork is tender and easily shreds with a fork.
- Remove the pork from the slow cooker and shred it using two forks. Return the shredded pork to the slow cooker and mix it with the juices.

2. **Prepare the Fries:**
   - Preheat your oven to 425°F (220°C).
   - Toss the cut potatoes with vegetable oil, salt, and pepper.
   - Spread the fries in a single layer on a baking sheet.
   - Bake for 25-30 minutes, or until crispy and golden brown, flipping halfway through.

3. **Make the Gravy:**
   - In a saucepan, melt the butter over medium heat.
   - Stir in the flour and cook for 1-2 minutes to form a roux.
   - Gradually whisk in the beef or chicken broth, and cook until the gravy thickens, about 5 minutes.
   - Season with salt and pepper to taste.

4. **Assemble the Poutine:**
   - Place the hot fries on a serving platter or individual plates.
   - Sprinkle the cheese curds over the fries.
   - Spoon the pulled pork evenly over the cheese curds.
   - Pour the hot gravy over the entire dish, allowing it to melt the cheese curds and coat the fries.
   - Garnish with chopped fresh parsley if desired.

5. **Serve:**
   - Serve the poutine immediately while hot and enjoy!

This Poutine with Pulled Pork is a decadent and satisfying meal, perfect for special occasions or whenever you're craving a comforting dish with a Canadian twist.

Cucumber and Dill Sandwiches

Ingredients:

- 1/2 cup cream cheese, softened
- 2 tablespoons unsalted butter, softened
- 1 tablespoon fresh dill, finely chopped (plus extra for garnish)
- 1 tablespoon lemon juice
- Salt and freshly ground black pepper, to taste
- 1 cucumber, thinly sliced
- 8 slices of white or whole wheat bread (preferably thinly sliced or crustless)
- Optional: 1 teaspoon chopped fresh chives or scallions

Instructions:

1. **Prepare the Spread:**
   - In a small bowl, combine the softened cream cheese and butter. Mix until smooth and well combined.
   - Stir in the chopped dill, lemon juice, and a pinch of salt and pepper. Adjust seasoning to taste.
   - If using, mix in the chopped chives or scallions for extra flavor.
2. **Prepare the Cucumbers:**
   - Peel the cucumber if desired (leaving the skin on is optional).
   - Slice the cucumber very thinly, ideally using a mandoline slicer for even, thin slices.
   - Lightly salt the cucumber slices and let them sit for 5 minutes to draw out excess moisture. Pat them dry with paper towels.
3. **Assemble the Sandwiches:**
   - Spread a generous layer of the dill cream cheese mixture on each slice of bread.
   - Arrange the cucumber slices evenly over half of the bread slices.
   - Top with the remaining slices of bread to form sandwiches.
   - For a neater presentation, trim the crusts off the sandwiches if desired.
4. **Slice and Serve:**
   - Cut the sandwiches into quarters or halves, depending on your preference.
   - Garnish with additional fresh dill if desired.
5. **Serve:**
   - Arrange the sandwiches on a platter and serve immediately, or cover with a damp cloth and refrigerate until ready to serve.

These Cucumber and Dill Sandwiches are light, flavorful, and perfect for any occasion where you want to offer a touch of elegance and freshness. Enjoy!

Duck Confit Sandwich

Ingredients:

For the Duck Confit:

- 2 duck legs (or about 1 1/2 to 2 pounds of duck confit)
- 1 tablespoon olive oil (if needed, for crisping)

For the Sandwich:

- 4 crusty rolls or ciabatta buns
- 1/2 cup mayonnaise
- 1 tablespoon Dijon mustard
- 1 tablespoon whole grain mustard (optional)
- 1 tablespoon chopped fresh parsley or chives (optional)
- 1 cup arugula or baby spinach
- 1/2 cup thinly sliced red onions
- 1/2 cup sliced pickles or cornichons
- 1/2 cup shredded Gruyère or Swiss cheese (optional)
- 1 apple, thinly sliced (optional, for added sweetness and crunch)
- Salt and freshly ground black pepper, to taste

Instructions:

1. **Prepare the Duck Confit:**
   - If using store-bought duck confit, remove the duck legs from their packaging and carefully remove the skin and bones.
   - Shred the duck meat with a fork, discarding any excess fat.
   - Heat a skillet over medium-high heat. If needed, add a tablespoon of olive oil to the skillet.
   - Add the shredded duck meat and cook for a few minutes, stirring occasionally, until the duck is heated through and slightly crispy.
2. **Prepare the Sandwich Spread:**
   - In a small bowl, mix together the mayonnaise, Dijon mustard, whole grain mustard (if using), and chopped parsley or chives (if desired). Season with salt and pepper to taste.
3. **Assemble the Sandwiches:**
   - Slice the rolls or ciabatta buns in half.
   - Spread a generous layer of the mustard-mayo mixture on the cut sides of each roll.
   - Top the bottom half of each roll with a portion of the shredded duck confit.
   - Add a handful of arugula or baby spinach.

- Layer on the sliced red onions, pickles or cornichons, and shredded cheese (if using).
- Arrange apple slices on top if desired.

4. **Finish and Serve:**
   - Top with the other half of the roll.
   - If you like, you can lightly toast the sandwiches in a panini press or on a skillet for a few minutes, until the cheese is melted and the rolls are crispy.

5. **Serve:**
   - Cut the sandwiches in half and serve warm.

These Duck Confit Sandwiches offer a delightful mix of flavors and textures, from the savory duck to the crisp greens and tangy mustard spread. Enjoy this gourmet treat!